Nobody Nowhere

Nobody Nowhere

||||

The Extraordinary

Autobiography

of an Autistic

Donna Williams

DOUBLEDAY CANADA LIMITED

Originally published in Great Britain by Doubleday, a division of Transworld Publishers Ltd., London.

Canadian Cataloguing in Publication Data

Williams, Donna, 1963–
Nobody nowhere

ISBN 0-385-25372-9

1. Williams, Donna, 1963–   2. Autism—Patients—Biography.   I. Title.

RC553.A88W55 1992   616.89′82′0092   C92-094402-7

Manufactured in the United States of America on acid-free paper
2   4   6   8   9   7   5   3
Book design by Susan Hood

Published in Canada by
Doubleday Canada Limited
105 Bond Street
Toronto, Ontario
M5B 1Y3

To Sharon, my grandparents, and the
Lawries of the world for simply being

Special thanks to Dr. Lawrie Bartak and the
Morgans for helping me to refine the lines of
communication

In a room without windows, in the company of shadows,
You know **they** won't forget you, they'll take you in.
Emotionally shattered, don't ask if it mattered,
Don't let it upset you, just start again.

In a world under glass, you can watch the world pass,
And nobody can touch you, you think you are safe.
But the wind can blow cold, in the depths of your soul,
Where you think nothing can hurt you till it is too late.

Run till you drop, do you know how to stop?
All the people walk right past you, you wave goodbye.
They all merely smiled, for you looked like a child
Never thought that they'd upset you, they saw you cry.

So take advice, don't question the experts.
Don't think twice, you just might listen,
Run and hide, to the corners of your mind, alone,
Like a nobody nowhere.

Foreword

This is truly a remarkable book. Donna Williams, against incredible odds, has written a masterpiece—a haunting, insightful, and electrifying account of her journey from a childhood as a severely withdrawn and bewildered autistic toddler to a university-educated successful writer.

Nobody Nowhere is exceptional in many ways. Most remarkable, in my view, is the journey itself. Very few have made the almost superhuman transition from autism to near-normalcy. Also remarkable is the author's superlative skill as a writer. Her inventive use of words and images verges on uncanny. Her candor, her incredible graciousness and naïveté in uncritically and uncomplainingly recounting her mistreatment by other people (some of whom were quite villainous), qualifies Donna Williams for near-sainthood.

Nobody Nowhere will be devoured by many readers. None will read it more avidly than those, like myself, with a consuming passion for learning about autism. As a research psychologist and the father of an autistic son, now thirty-six, I have read everything I could find on autism for well over three decades. There is nothing quite like Donna Williams's story for gaining so clear a picture of life as seen through the eyes of an autistic child. Donna Williams was not the typical autistic child—there *is* no typical autistic child, just as there is no typical reader of her book. But Donna Williams's account of the world as she experienced it provides us with as good a description of "autism from the inside" as we are ever likely to get. I have not yet recovered from my astonishment at being so close, after all these years, to understanding—almost experiencing—parts of the life of an autistic person, albeit a very high-functioning, highly gifted autistic person.

Much of what Donna Williams has written about the experience of autism was already familiar to me—at an intellectual level. But *Nobody Nowhere* provides a heretofore unavailable—and alarming—highly subjective appreciation of what it is like to be autistic.

What causes autism? Donna has been studying it for a decade; I have been seeking answers for several decades. We have been looking in different places, in different ways, but we have arrived at some similar answers. Donna reports that many (not all) of her symptoms were traceable to certain food allergies, and that her brain reacted badly when its vitamin supply was insufficient. I encountered my first case of milk-allergy-caused autism in 1967, and have since become aware of hundreds of children whose behavior greatly improves when cow's milk, wheat, eggs, or other common foods are removed from their diet. As for vitamins: There are now sixteen studies in the world literature (two of them by me) showing that almost half of all autistic children and adults need larger amounts of vitamin B_6 and the mineral magnesium than do nonautistic persons. (Donna's editor tells me Donna was astonished to come upon my writings on these topics.) Part of the problem of autism, in many autistic persons, is thus obviously *biochemical*.

Researchers in neuroanatomy are also discovering subtle *structural* anomalies in the brains of some autistic persons, especially in the cerebellar circuits that permit the normal brain to select, prioritize, and process information effectively. When these circuits malfunction, the automatic shifts of attention that make life flow smoothly for normal infants and children are grossly impaired in the autistic child, so that he or she becomes oblivious to many of the social cues and to the constant stream of cause-and-effect sequences that give coherence and meaning to normal experience.

The agonizing difficulties in the autistic person's ability to sort and process information, in my opinion, not only underlie many of the deficits of autism, but may also account for the islets of brilliance, or savant abilities, manifested by so many autistic persons, including Donna Williams.

The nature of the autistic person's attentional mechanisms strongly predispose him or her to "tune out" the multitude of ongoing events that serve to distract the nonautistic mind. Thus the autistic person is enabled (perhaps even compelled) to remain concentrated on such tasks as multiplying large numbers mentally or memorizing phone books.

Nobody Nowhere sheds long-needed light on one of the great mysteries of autism: the process of recovery. Judging from the clear example of Donna Williams, the autistic person must first improve enough and be perceptive enough to recognize him- or herself as non-normal in some detail. Beyond this, the person must be intensely motivated to strive *hard* to overcome the difficulty. (My own autistic son, Mark, while now relatively high-functioning, does not have such motivation. He seems quite content with his life.)

One of the most interesting parts of *Nobody Nowhere* is the author's account of why she wrote the book. We have known for decades that autistic persons experience life as an incoherent series of unconnected events. By putting her chaotic life experiences on paper, in chronological order, Donna hoped to construct a coherent picture in her own mind of who she was. After that, the book was to have been burned! What a tragedy that would have been!

Recovery, when it takes place, is not an automatic process. One of the techniques currently used by skilled teachers is behavior modification, the reward-and-punishment process that worked so well with Helen Keller, to teach autistic children many of the simple things, such as the colors and the alphabet, that normal children learn by osmosis. But this straightforward teaching procedure often brings about surprisingly great improvement in the child's overall behavior, especially if the teaching is started before about age five. In my view, the reason for the unexpected progress in these autistic children is that the process teaches them, in addition to the letters A B C, that they *can and must pay attention* when, despite their best efforts, the child cannot grasp *why* he or she must. Sometimes, even if the world seems chaotic, *if* you pay close attention to the fragments, *and* you strive hard to piece them together, you have a good chance for real improvement. This has worked for many autistic children (the lucky ones) and, quite possibly, it was one of the factors that helped Donna Williams. Perhaps under these conditions, autism, the experiential jigsaw puzzle, may have a solution.

Nobody Nowhere helps beautifully to fill an important gap in our knowledge of autism. A multitude of gaps remain. There is much to learn.

Bernard Rimland, Ph.D.
Director, Autism Research Institute
San Diego, California
June 1992

Introduction

This book is a fascinating, courageous story about a young woman's early life. Donna Williams has autism and yet has managed to develop into a perceptive and thoughtful adult who has the ability to look at her own reactions and write about them in a manner that is accurate and detached and at the same time intensely personal and full of feeling. *Nobody Nowhere* is an exceptional achievement for many reasons. As a result of her autism, and in spite of her rich insights and her skill in writing about them, Donna has considerable difficulty understanding her own and other people's behavior in everyday situations. Life is still an enormous struggle for her, and she continues to be handicapped in many ways.

At one level, Donna's story is simply a heartwarming and heartrending account of a girl's development in difficult circumstances that will grip the ordinary reader's attention. Most of us will be able to identify with the uncertainties of childhood and adolescence she describes. At another level, the book has many insights for the professional who is involved with child development and the treatment of its distortions. Finally, the book is unique in that it provides an exceptional resource for the professional who works with people with autism. Autistic people cannot usually describe how they feel, and others are nearly always limited to an interpretation of their behavior. Professionals are not super-human and are just as prone to making incorrect, if not downright silly, interpretations of what they observe as any-body else. Many of the things we notice in people with au-tism remain puzzling, even after some forty to fifty years of research in this field. Donna's skill, humor, and good sense, which shine through in this book, therefore provide an abundance of useful insights for the professional who is trying to help people with autism cope more adequately with their environment.

I have worked with autistic people for twenty-five years and have often discovered autism in both children and adults where it had not been previously suspected. I have also had the happier experience of concluding that some-body did not have autism after they had been sent to me for advice and assistance on the assumption that they were af-flicted with it. When Donna first contacted me and told me she had been said to be autistic and would like my help, I agreed to meet her, even though I thought it quite possible that she did not have autism but was emotionally disturbed in some way. It is quite clear, however, that she does have autism, and all the evidence clearly indicates that she has been autistic since an early age.

Autism is a rare but troubling disorder. About four chil-dren out of every ten thousand develop it, and most of these are boys. Approximately one child in five with autism is female, so that in a population of sixty million—roughly one quarter the size of the United States—there would be about five thousand females of all ages with autism. In contrast, two or three hundred thousand females in the same popu-lation would have some degree of mental handicap.

While there are many things we do not know about au-tism, there are a few things we do know with reasonable certainty. It is not caused by bad parenting, but rather is the result of some abnormality of brain development occurring for a variety of reasons either before birth or early in child-hood. People with autism are not necessarily mentally hand-icapped and, generally speaking, are relatively able to do certain kinds of tasks, although they have severe difficulty in a few characteristic areas. On the whole, they get through life by rote, learning rules for dealing with situations but often having very little understanding of the meaning and significance of what they are dealing with. They also find it hard to process information about people and their relationships. This can vary from an inability to recognize facial expressions or even to know which parts of the face tell us what someone is feeling, to a general difficulty in understanding what is going on in common social situations and in recognizing what someone is feeling from their tone of voice, choice of words, and other cues in normal conversation.

A third major area of difficulty is the comprehension of any information expressed through spoken language. Autistic children are commonly thought to be deaf because they are unresponsive to other people's speech. However, aural tests show that they can hear, and other tests indicate that the problem lies in a severe delay in the development of their ability to understand speech. In spite of these problems, which make the world seem an extremely perplexing and frightening place, such children are often very interested in their surroundings and may display surprising skill in manipulating objects—for instance, completing jigsaw puzzles on the basis of the shapes of the pieces and with no help from the picture, which they are generally unable to interpret.

The problems described here lead people with autism to display three major kinds of behavior. In the first place, they are emotionally unresponsive and sometimes actively avoid relating to people. In babies, this is often shown by failure to maintain eye contact with a parent or to display feeling through facial expressions. In older children, it may be indicated by the child's failure to make friends or to be able to play in the company of other children. Second, they are relatively unresponsive to other people's speech and may have impaired, abnormal, or little or no speech of their own. Children with autism often speak with a monotonous or oddly pitched tone of voice and frequently echo things said to them. Third, they display rigid, stereotyped behavior in which they may insist on a very unchanging environment or carry out repetitive, purposeless activities such as lining objects up repeatedly or counting things over and over again. Attempts by others to interrupt such children's routines or to change their environment make them quite distressed. This distress may result in intense displays of temper, with children biting themselves, repeatedly striking their heads against walls, or punching themselves to a degree sufficient to produce severe injury.

While Donna has displayed all these principal features of autism, she is nevertheless very unusual. She is exceptionally intelligent, which means that although she is relatively impaired in her grasp of language, she is able to converse simply with other people for short periods in favorable circumstances. She is fortunate in that her language impairment is least marked in the area of written expression. This means that, although she still has some difficulty in speaking, understanding other people's speech, and understanding written material, she can express herself clearly in her own writing. Her difficulties in understanding other people's behavior are characteristically autistic, but she does comprehend that other people interact in some mysterious way, and she is motivated to try and learn to be like them. Thus, she has been able to write this book in spite of her continuing autism.

Even though it sometimes seems overwhelming to parents and professionals trying to deal with it, autism is not the sole characteristic of a person afflicted with it. People with autism vary as enormously as any other group of people; they may be bright or dull, cheerful or difficult, mischievous or compliant, and so on. Much of the behavior shown by people with autism consists of normal reactions to an environment that seems decidedly odd to them and that indeed may be odd in reality. Apart from their autism, autistic people may be emotionally disturbed or relatively well adjusted, just like any other people. It is very clear, both from this book and from my personal acquaintance with Donna, that she is a surprisingly strong person with much compassion. She is certainly not emotionally disturbed, despite the opinions expressed about her over many years. She is not mad and never has been, and she has an unexpected ability to maintain a realistic and commonsense view about so many things.

Among Donna's many surprising qualities are her tenacity and perseverance in trying to improve her lot in whatever circumstances she finds herself, and her uncanny ability to reflect upon her own behavior and that of others. That she is able to reason in this way and yet continue to have considerable difficulty in relating to people is extremely unusual. It is perhaps just another reflection of the exceptional intelligence that has enabled her to cope in situations where her emotions have not been sufficiently developed to allow her to rely on them in the unthinking and spontaneous way that other people do.

This is a story of relevance to everybody, especially those who have had to contend with difficulties in growing up. Donna is a very normal person who has autism and has learned to cope with it, for the most part. She still does not understand why other people do many of the things they do with each other and why they would want to. She does, however, know that she is determined to learn more about these things and hopes she will come to enjoy them as other people seem to. In pursuit of her aims, Donna writes regularly to a number of other people with autism around the world. Understandably, in view of her experiences and disability, there are a number of activities that she finds extremely difficult, such as touching others physically and being with people in unfamiliar rooms. Nevertheless, recognizing that she need not fear things that she can see others enjoy with little difficulty, she has actively subjected herself to such frightening experiences. It is in such recent efforts of hers, as well as in the many examples throughout this book, that we can see how brave a person Donna is.

Nobody Nowhere does us all a great service. It reminds us

all what it means to be human. It is a moving and fascinating story of a life still beginning. It brings a wealth of insights about being disabled and about being courageous. It offers an abundance of help for professionals working with children and young adults, and will illuminate many of their puzzling experiences in working with autistic children. It gives graphic insights into the stress experienced by families of autistic children and shows clearly that it is possible for the family of someone with autism to be disturbed in various ways and yet for this disturbance to have no relevance to the causes of autism in the child. Parents of autistic children may be less or more disturbed than any other parents and should be free to be so without any unjustified accusations that they have caused their child's autism because of their own difficulties. Although it is possible that with a more favorable background she might have developed to her present level earlier, it is clear that Donna eventually would have been as well adjusted as she is whatever her family circumstances had been. Speculation apart, this book provides a clear account of a disabled child living with a disturbed family situation without the two sets of unfortunate circumstances being necessarily connected. Donna is clear about this, far more so than many professionals in the field, much to their discredit and the misfortune of their clients.

Nobody Nowhere is a triumph. Read it and share in Donna Williams's battle, the immensely successful way she has been able to allow her humanity to outweigh her problems, and the lucid and absorbing story she presents.

Lawrence Bartak, M.A., Ph.D.,
 C. Psychol., F.A.Ps.S., A.F.B.Ps.S.
Senior Lecturer in Psychology
 and Special Education,
 Monash University, Australia

Author's Note

This is a story of two battles, a battle to keep out "the world" and a battle to join it. It tells of the battles within my own world and the battle lines, tactics used, and casualties of my private war against others.

This is my attempt at a truce, the conditions of which are on my terms. I have, throughout my private war, been a she, a you, a Donna, a me, and finally, an I. All of us will tell it like it was and like it is.

If you sense distance, you're not mistaken; it's real. Welcome to *my* world.

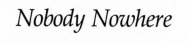

Nobody Nowhere

I remember my first dream—or, at least, the first that I can recall. I was moving through white, with no objects, just white. Bright spots of fluffy color surrounded me everywhere. I passed through them, and they passed through me. It was the sort of thing that made me laugh.

This dream came before any others with shit or people or monsters in them, and certainly before I noticed the difference between the three. I must have been less than three years old. This dream depicted the nature of my world at that time. Awake, I pursued the dream relentlessly. I would face the light shining through the window next to my cot and rub my eyes furiously. There they were. The bright fluffy colors moving through the white. "Stop that!" came the intrusive gabble. I'd continue rubbing merrily. *Slap.*

I discovered the air was full of spots. If you looked into nothingness, there were spots. People would walk by, obstructing my magical view of nothingness. I'd move past them. They'd gabble. My attention would be firmly set on my desire to lose myself in the spots, and I'd ignore the gabble, looking straight through this obstruction with a calm expression, soothed by being lost in the spots. *Slap.* I was learning about "the world."

I learned eventually to lose myself in anything I desired—

the patterns on the wallpaper or the carpet, the sound of something over and over again, like the hollow thud I'd get from tapping my chin. Even people became no problem. Their words became a mumbling jumble, their voices a pattern of sounds. I could look through them until I wasn't there, and then, later, I learned to lose myself *in them.*

Words were no problem, but other people's expectations for me to respond to them were. This would have required my understanding what was said, but I was too happy losing myself to want to be dragged back by something as two-dimensional as understanding.

"What do you think you're doing?" came the voice.

Knowing I must respond in order to get rid of this annoyance, I would compromise, repeating "What do you think you're doing?" addressed to no one in particular.

"Don't repeat everything I say," scolded the voice.

Sensing a need to respond, I'd reply: "Don't repeat everything I say."

Slap. I had no idea what was expected of me.

For the first three and a half years of my life this was my language, complete with the intonation and inflection of those I came to think of as "the world." The world seemed to be impatient, annoying, callous, and unrelenting. I learned to respond to it as such, crying, squealing, ignoring it, and running away.

Once, instead of simply "hearing" a particular sentence, I truly understood it because it had *significance* for me. I was three and a half. My parents were visiting some friends, and I was standing in the hall outside the living room. I was giving myself whizzies—arms outstretched, spinning around and around. I have a vague recollection that there were other children there, for the topic of discussion in the living room had disturbed and embarrassed me. A question was asked about my toilet training. My mother replied that I was still wetting myself.

I don't know whether this had done the trick, but I became more aware of needing to go to the toilet. I certainly had a great fear of going to the toilet at this time. I would hold on for what seemed like forever, and then go just before I did it on the spot. Sometimes I would hold on for several days until I was so constipated that I would vomit up bile. Then I became afraid of eating food, too. I would eat only custard, jelly, baby-food, fruit, lettuce leaves, honey, and white pieces of bread with multicolored "hundreds and thousands" sprinkled on top, like the spots of color in my dream. In fact I ate the things that I liked to look at and feel or that had nice associations for me more than anything else. Rabbits ate lettuce. I loved fluffy rabbits. I ate lettuce. I loved colored glass. Jelly was like that. I loved jelly. Like other children, I ate dirt and flowers and grass and bits of plastic. Unlike other children, I still ate flowers, grass, bark, and plastic when I was thirteen years old. As a teenager, the old rules still applied. If I liked something, I would try to lose myself in my fascination for it. Things, unlike people, were welcome to become a part of me.

When I was about three, I had signs of malnutrition. Though not skeletal, I had bluish skin and would bruise at the slightest touch. My eyelashes would come out in large clumps, and my gums bled. My parents thought I had leukemia and took me for a blood test. The doctor took some blood from my earlobe. I cooperated. I was intrigued by a multicolored cardboard wheel the doctor had given me. I also had hearing tests because, although I mimicked everything, it appeared that I was deaf. My parents would stand behind me and make sudden loud noises without my so much as blinking in response. "The world" simply wasn't getting in.

> *I thought I felt a whisper through my soul,*
> *Everything is nothing, and nothing is everything.*
> *Death in life and life in death of falsity.*

The more I became aware of the world around me, the more I became afraid. Other people were my enemies, and reaching out to me was their weapon, with only a few exceptions —my grandparents, my father, and my Aunty Linda.

I still remember the smell of my grandmother. She wore chains around her neck. She was soft and wrinkly, wore knitted things that I could put my fingers through, had a husky, laughing voice, and smelled of camphor. I would take camphor off the shelves at the supermarket, and twenty years later bought bottle upon bottle of eucalyptus oil and spread it around my room, corner to corner, to keep out everything else except for the comforting feeling that association gave me. I collected scraps of colored wool and crocheted bits and would put my fingers through the holes so that I could fall asleep securely. For me, the people I liked *were* their things, and those things (or things like them) were my protection from the things I didn't like—other people.

The habits I adopted of keeping and manipulating these symbols were my equivalent of magic spells cast against the nasties who could invade me if I lost my cherished objects or had them taken away. My strategies were not the result of insanity or hallucination, but simply harmless imagination made potent by my overwhelming fear of vulnerability.

IIII

MY GRANDFATHER FED me raisins and biscuits, piece by piece. He made up special names for everything; he sure knew his audience. He understood my world and so was able to fascinate me with his. He had some liquid mercury balls that he would splatter into tinier balls and make chase one another. He had two minute magnetized Scottie dogs, which he would make chase one another as well. This sort of chasing was safe. Communication via objects was safe. Special names for everything, so that it was "our little world"—that was safe. Every morning while it was still semidark I would go out to the shack in which he lived.

One day I went out to my grandfather's shack. He didn't notice me. His face was purple and blotchy. He was lying on his side. Pop never woke up again. I never forgave him for doing this until I was twenty-one, when it suddenly dawned on me that people don't intentionally mean to die.

Then I cried, and I cried, and I cried some more; it had taken me sixteen years to grieve for him.

||||

MY FATHER STOPPED existing when I was about three. Up till then, he—like my grandfather—intrigued me by calling things by special names. There was a man he called Cyril the fox, all cats became Brookenstein, Charlie Warmton was the bed, and I was Polly the Possum or Miss Polly. He had actually called me this because I was echolalic till I was four, repeating meaninglessly everything I heard, just like a parrot.

My father catered to my fascination for small fancy things and shiny objects. He would bring me something different every week and would always build me up by asking me if I knew how special and magical these various bits and bobs were. I would sit on his knee, my eyes fastened to the object, listening to the story as though he were one of my storytelling records. In my head I would do the introduction: "This is an original little long-playing record, and I am your storyteller. We are going to begin now to read the story of . . ." I still have those treasures, twenty-three years later. Then he —who he was—deserted me, at least figuratively. When I found another he whom I liked, many years later, it took me several years to make the connection that these two people were in fact the same person.

||||

MY MOTHER WAS as hard as I was gentle, though strangely we shared the same distant and unreachable nature.

She had wanted to put me in a children's home, and I recall being terrified and hysterical, kicking my feet against the car as she tried many times to force me in. I knew the terror of what else she could dish out, and if being sent to a home was the last resort, then I thought that surely must be an insufferable torture comparable to hell on earth. When my mother spoke, the room shook. You listened, even if you did not hear.

I had an older brother. I think he became her "only" child. Perhaps she wanted a daughter, for she would dress my brother up as a girl and a boy on alternate days and take him out for walks in the pram. We were both pretty children, but he could "act normal" and was not so embarrassing.

I am sure my father thwarted her efforts by giving my grandparents the responsibility for me. Perhaps, too, they had tried to reach me and persisted beyond the point where her hope had run out. Nevertheless, my father paid the price for this, as did their relationship. He was ordered not to speak to me and to have nothing to do with me.

||||

ADMITTEDLY MY FATHER was as insensitive and indifferent to my mother and my older brother as she was to me. The family was split straight down the middle, spiraling into a downward decline before crashing headlong into the pits of hell.

It became a chain reaction. The tension would explode, he would degrade and abuse her, and she would degrade and abuse me. Both of them had found forms of escape that persisted on and off over many years, leaving in their wake more destructiveness than I could ever have conjured up in the magic of my insular little world.

I never hugged either of them; neither was I hugged. I didn't like anyone coming too close to me, let alone touching me. I felt that all touching was pain, and I was frightened.

||||

MY MOTHER WAS a person who, although she had no friends to impress, took pride in how her children looked. So she would brush my hair. I had long, curly blond hair, and she would tear through it and its many knots with a vengeance.

My Aunty Linda also loved to brush my hair, though she

would do it so lightly that I would find it annoying. "Am I hurting you?" she would say, as though I were some breakable china doll. "Harder," I would order. And, though careful not to tear through the knots, she would sit there brushing my hair for ages, and I would sit there enjoying *feeling* it. "You have fairy hair," she would say, "so silky, and look at the way it fluffs out." I liked the words that she used and thought about the feel of such things. For many years I played with, touched, and chewed on my own hair. Touching other children's hair was the only friendly physical contact I would make.

> *The wisps surround me in my bed,*
> *They hover there for to protect me;*
> *For the wisps, they are my friends.*

People were forever saying that I had no friends. In fact my world was full of them. They were far more magical, reliable, predictable, and real than other children, *and* they came with guarantees. It was a world of my own creation where I didn't need to control myself or the objects, animals, and nature, which were simply *being* in my presence. I had two other friends who did not belong to this physical world: the wisps, and a pair of green eyes named Willie that hid under my bed.

I was afraid to sleep, always had been. I would sleep with my eyes open, and I did this for years. I guess I did not appear to be terribly normal. "Haunting" or "haunted" would have been better adjectives. I was afraid of the dark, though I loved the early dusk and dawn.

My earliest memory of the wisps was when I began to sleep in a bed. It must have been in the new house we lived in, though the old one had, in my mind, blended into this one. It was as though it was now a series of rooms that I could no longer find within the new house. This disturbed me. I liked to know where everything was—including my parents. I had to know where everyone was and that they were all sleeping before I could go to sleep. I would lie in bed, stiff and silent, listening for an end to the muffled household sounds around me, as I watched the transparent wisps hovering over me.

The wisps were tiny creatures, almost transparent. They hung in the air directly above me, and looked something like wisps of hair, which is probably where my mind had found the idea.

My bed was also surrounded and totally encased by tiny spots that I called stars, so that it seemed to me I lay in some kind of mystical glass coffin. (I have since learned that they are actually air particles, yet my vision was so hypersensitive that they often became a hypnotic foreground with the rest of "the world" fading away.) By looking through the stars and not at them, I could see them, and the rule was that I could not close my eyes or they would depart, leaving me unprotected against intruders coming into the room. Feeling safe was a tiring business.

And the intruders came. They were responsible for taking away my protection, for in the change of focus the tiny spots would disappear, leaving me feeling angry and betrayed, alone, exposed, and vulnerable.

I knew that people were disturbed at me sleeping with my eyes open. I soon learned to close them when I heard others coming, to play dead and never look at them or let anything register when they lifted my eyelids or even poked me in the eye. I was breathing, so they knew I wasn't dead.

The wisps left me by the time I had started "proper" school, though the stars around me as I slept (probably a later version of the spots) persisted on and off, and sometimes still appear.

||||

WILLIE WAS ANOTHER story. Willie had begun at the same time as the wisps. I was probably about two years old. Unlike the wisps, he gave me no comfort, but he was a form of protection against intruders in the night. He was no more than a pair of piercing green eyes that could only be seen in the darkness. I was frightened of him, but so, I thought, were they; and so, come hell or high water, I sided with this character. As with anything I became close to, I would try to lose myself within it. I took to sleeping under the bed and I became Willie.

By this time I was three years old. Willie became the self I directed at the outside world, complete with hateful glaring eyes, a pinched-up mouth, a rigid corpselike stance, and clenched fists. Willie stamped his foot, Willie spat when he didn't like things, but the look of complete hatred was the worst weapon and Donna paid the price. His name was probably derived from my own surname, and some of Willie's behavior was certainly modeled upon and in response to my violator: my mother.

Willie learned to turn other people's phrases back at them in some sort of meaningful yet attacking way, though silence still seemed a far deadlier weapon. My mother began to think I was evil and possessed. It would have been easier to forgive her if she had suffered from some kind of mental illness. She didn't. Her lack of education and upbringing, her isolation and her drinking, accounted for these beliefs more in terms of explanation than of delusion.

IIII

MY MOTHER HAD retreated into a world of her own; but, unlike mine, it held no safety for her. Her only salvation and her only friend was my brother. It was a war in which I was to fight alone. They sided together, and together they would gang up on me.

To them, I was a nut, a retard, a spastic. I threw "mentals" and couldn't act normal. "Look at her, look at her," they would say about a child who, to them, was either "a retard" when I was in my own world or "a nut" when I was in theirs. I couldn't win.

Looking at it from their point of view, I guess they couldn't win, either. My brother had probably woken up to the fact that I hardly acknowledged, let alone accepted, him, and my mother had long since been robbed of a life and the pride she so badly needed, which had been lacking long before I ever came along. She cast herself as the tormented single mother. My brother became the too-important only child. And, as their accusations flew at me, so, too, did the accusations fly at them from everyone else.

People were saying that she had caused me to be so withdrawn by her coldness and her violence. She probably believed this, and I let her. Had I ever wanted to reach out as myself to the intrusive outside world, I am sure she would have inhibited me. Some battered children form attachments with such a parent. I never did.

If I wanted a war, I guess I won. Though she was probably a social cripple before I was born, I accept my share of the responsibility for making her one, and for robbing both her and my brother of a free, more independent relationship with each other, which has resulted in his rejection of her all these years later.

When my mother had fought to put me in an institution and my father had fought to keep me at home, each must have had his or her own conception of the future. Each was right. I became a rewarding experience for my father. I became my mother's hell. She called me Dolly, the doll she never had. In her own words I learned who I was: "You were my doll, and I was allowed to smash it," she told me over and over again. My mother had but one reward. I was also to be her little dancing doll.

||||

WHEN I WAS three, my mother took me to my first dancing lesson. I walked on tiptoe, loved classical music, and would make up dances by myself for myself, and this was taken as an indication that I would do well at ballet. I loved pretty things and accepted the ribbons and netting and sequins. Wearing them made them part of me; I had no objections. Other people wanting to take a part of this from me to share it was another matter altogether.

I remember the low cyclone fencing outside the weather-board hall in which I was to give one of my first and last public performances for a long time. I remember the dirt path that had worn down in the middle of the grass strip we were walking along. It was probably a driveway, but this was how I saw things: bit by bit, a string of pieces strung together.

We went up a few steps and through the double wooden doors. I was captured by the room, by the wood and by the smoothness of the floor. My mother was probably fantasizing about how much she had longed to be in my shoes when she was a child.

||||

MY MOTHER WAS the second of nine children, and the second daughter. Her family was poor, and instead of distributing what little extras they got among all of the children, the eldest daughter seemed to get it all.

The Salvation Army entertained the others while the eldest daughter got dolls, pretty clothes, and dancing lessons. My mother had watched her older sister in hate and awe. She gave up competing and tried for the role of the eldest boy and won it. It was not as glorious, not as glamorous, and built little sense of self-worth, but it gave her position and the satisfaction of violently thumping her older sister and the friends she never made.

My mother's sister thrived on the attention she got, becoming charismatic and a charmer. Ultimately she paid in guilt and shame, reaching out for forgiveness from her younger sister, who greeted this with the same amount of mercy she got from me: none.

||||

INSIDE THE PERFORMANCE hall it seemed that there were children everywhere. Pink arms and legs protruded from torsos clad in Willoughby Dancing School black leotards. The rowdy rabble began to subside as the sharpness of the instructor's voice broke through.

The children lined up to form a big square. "Eyes to the front." "No, you move over to the left." "No, not right, left." "Look, you stand here." Helpful invasive arms, instructing, interfering. Me looking at my feet. The walls were going up.

The music was a blur. There was too much turmoil going on around me, invading my space and invading my mind. With clenched fists, I stamped my foot and spat several times upon the floor. "Take her out of here, Mrs. Williams," said Mr. Willoughby, the teacher. "I am afraid she is not ready yet. Bring her back in a couple of years."

Ashamed, my mother's dreams and hopes exploded in her own face. I was looking at the floor. My arm was being tugged violently. I was looking up. Words poured out of her mouth, the tone was deadly. "That's it. You're going to a home."

The hysterics went on in my head and probably spewed forth into the car, though I was not aware. Willie never made it as a ballerina.

My mother began to see me, not as herself anymore, but as her spoiled sister. I became "Marion," and as if to stress her hatred, this came to be "Maggots."

> I see that girl in the mirror, looking back at me.
> I see her thinking I am crazy for believing I am free.
> Yet I can see it in her eyes that as I am staring,
> She is trying to understand that I am not lying,
> I am just trying to find my way back home to me.

There was a park at the end of our street, and there were roses on the way. There were houses, and every one of them had a special name. The house on the end was the "Rose House."

I'd leave the house in the early dawn and go exploring. I'd watch the fish in Mr. Smith's fish pond, peer though the glass doors at the back of the rose lady's house, dance in their gardens singing songs or reciting poems I'd picked up. I'd throw the rose lady's rose petals high into the air and walk through them as though they were the stars around my bed. Perhaps I was an angel to watch, but I was a devil to try to be with. The rose lady never told me off for the roses. Someone once commented on my singing. I then stopped singing in front of people, although I didn't realize for many years that they could still hear me even if I couldn't see them.

IIII

THE PARK WAS a magical place. I would lie in the middle of the seesaw, making it tip up and down. On the swing I could make my neighbor Lina's backyard appear and disappear, which made me laugh. Sometimes Lina would come outside and see me. She would come to the park or ask me to come over. I would laugh and keep swinging higher and higher. *Look, no one can touch me.*

Lina and her mother spoke only Italian to each other, and I loved to hear her and her mother talk. They had gentle voices; even when authoritative they didn't sound hard.

I loved the smell of their house, and there were so many things to see and to see through. Crystal glasses lined polished streaky teak cabinets and stood upon mirrored shelves as though, deservedly, they were on stage. The floor was smooth and shiny like silk. It looked good enough to eat. Everything seemed nice to touch. I'd rub my cheek against the curtains, the cabinets, the seat covers, and the glass door.

Lina's mother thought I was beautiful and fed me pieces of squid. I liked pieces of squid because I liked Lina's mother. And when she would laugh her eyes would dance and her whole body seemed to roll with the laugh.

I liked Lina. She had an older brother who was a bully. I understood that.

Lina's mother asked what had happened to her potted plants; they had bites taken out of them. I turned my head away and tried not to laugh. "Did you do that?" gestured Lina. I looked into her eyes, and my eyes didn't lie.

||||

MY FAVORITE TREE lived in the park. I would climb it and hang upside down by my knees and swing, usually from the highest branch I could find. Sometimes I would sing, sometimes I would hum. As long as everything moved to the rhythm, I was happy.

Sometimes I would suddenly flip myself out of the tree in some dramatic final swing. I would let my legs go from the tree and go flying before landing with a thud upon the ground. Sometimes I would knock the wind out of myself. I'd often be scratched. It made no difference. I'd get to my feet and continue on to the next adventure. Mine was a rich world, but like many rich people I was very alone.

One particular day, I was swinging from my tree. A girl approached me and began to talk to me as I swung. Her name was Carol. I guess I looked quite strange to her, as I was wearing only my white smocklike nightie, which was falling down over my head, leaving the rest of me exposed. My face must have shocked her even more, as I had painted it with patterns using my mother's makeup. I thought I was beautiful. I must have looked a mess.

I went with this giant of a girl. I was fascinated by her animation, though I hardly understood a word she said. I heard words. I probably copied them. But only her actions and their ability to capture me had any significance, and as long as things were new to me I was captured.

||||

WE WENT TO Carol's house. Her mother was shocked about the state of my colorful face. I was surprised by her shock; I thought the colors were delightful. Carol and her mother were laughing at me. People often did in my presence.

Later people would say they were laughing with me, not

at me, but I wasn't laughing. So I copied them, and made what they said correct. Then they would laugh at my strange laugh, and I would laugh with them, and they would think I was amused and amusing. This proved useful when I was older. I'd get invited back again. I was learning to perform.

Carol's mother got a washcloth and washed my face and hands and legs. There I was. All brand-new. She placed a drink in front of me. I looked at it, waiting to be told what to do. "You can drink it," said a voice. It was a sentence of words, a statement. I looked at the glass and at the mother and at the girl. The girl, sitting across the table, lifted her glass and drank. I was her mirror. I copied her.

"Where does she live?" said a voice.

"I don't know. I found her in the park," said another voice.

"I think you'd better take her back there," said the mother.

Fear came and took me away. I stopped being there.

Carol took me by the hand. She led me back to the park. My eyes, like a camera, captured the moment. She lived in another world within that house of hers. I wanted so much to be a part of it. I glared at her—betrayed. The world was throwing me out.

I had discovered choice. I wanted to live in Carol's world, in Carol's house. "Where do you live?" came her voice, as she slipped away from my reality. I stared at her, I screamed inside with frustration. No sound came out. I watched the person who had been Carol wave goodbye and say words. For many years, I wondered if she was real, for nobody had, till then, so totally held me within "the world." This stranger, who I only ever met once, was to change my life. She became "the girl in the mirror." Later I became Carol.

As I got older, I would compulsively bring home kitten after kitten, reenacting the way Carol had taken me home, and I would wait and wonder when my mother would become Carol's mother. She never did.

||||

I FINALLY GAVE up waiting for Carol to come back to the park. I didn't want to swing from my tree anymore. It hurt too much. I began to spend almost all of my time looking in the mirror.

There was a long mirror in my bedroom. In its reflection I could see my brother's bedroom door. My brother never came through this door. I assume that he either didn't sleep in there or that he made his way out through the other door, leading out onto the back porch. Had he come in there, I'm sure I would have screamed. My room was my world; my mother, though unwanted and uninvited, was the only intruder whose presence was tolerated.

In the day I wanted the door shut. In the night I wanted it open, to keep an eye on anything that might enter. Carol came in through the mirror.

Carol looked just like me, but the look in her eyes betrayed her identity. It was Carol all right. I began to talk to her, and she copied me. I was angry. I didn't expect her to do that. My expression asked her why, and hers asked me. I figured that the answer was a secret.

I decided that Carol understood that no one else was allowed to see me communicating with her and that this was her way of protecting me. I began to whisper to her, putting my face very close to hers and wondering why she didn't turn to hear.

When I was not in front of the mirror, Carol would disappear. I would feel deserted. When I walked in front of it, she would come back, and I'd try to look behind the mirror to find if she had gone through the door that I could see in the background. It wasn't the door to my brother's room after all. It was Carol's house! The room I saw her in, in the mirror, was only a room between her world and mine.

Now I understood the secret. If I could get through that room, I could leave with her, into her world. The only problem was how to get into the mirror.

I had realized that I had to walk straight into the mirror if I was ever to get into that room. For the next four years I tried. I would walk straight into it and wonder why I couldn't get through.

The anxiety of my inner battle was becoming unbearable. I could say words but I wanted to *communicate.* I wanted to express something. I wanted to let something out. The anxiety would have been so easy to give in to; whereby I would again lose all awareness of self and my surroundings.

I would cry and look desperately into Carol's eyes in the mirror, wanting to know the way out of my mental prison. I began to hit myself in frustration—slapping my own face, biting myself, and pulling out my hair. If my mother had not been so good at it, the abuse that I poured out on myself would have put her efforts to shame.

I had problems with people coming near me. I would flinch and move away. My father blamed my mother. My mother blamed her treatment of me on my behavior. My older brother, becoming more and more fed up with me, called me a spastic. I mirrored his obscene impersonations. *Slap.* I learned not to respond at all.

I eventually believed that it was the resistance I felt just before hitting the mirror that had stopped me from getting into Carol's world. I realize in retrospect how true this was. It was certainly some uncontrollable inner resistance that was stopping me from getting into the world in general.

I began to sit in a huddled ball inside the cupboard. I would close my eyes and try hard to lose all sensation of my own existence so that I could get into Carol's world in my mind. I became angry at any need to go to the toilet or eat, or any call to participate in the family (by fetching things, which was my main household role). In short my humanness, my mere physical existence, was my failing.

||||

IN THE DARKNESS of that cupboard I found Carol within myself.

Carol was everything that people liked. Carol laughed a lot. Carol made friends. Carol brought things home. Carol had a mother.

To my mother's delight, Carol could act relatively normal. Smiling, sociable, giggly, she made the perfect dancing doll, just in time to make Mr. Willoughby's prediction true: "Bring her back in a couple of years. She'll be ready then."

In the meantime, unable to accept that "the world" had won a round, Donna had disappeared. I was by this time five years old.

I hated calling anyone else by name, including myself. I never told them that I believed my name was Carol and that they were playing characters she met. Fear of betraying the secret was fear of losing the grip on Carol's world. It was that grip that was my only way out of my inner prison. I had created an ego detached from the self, which was still shackled by crippled emotions. It became more than an act. It became my life, and as I had to reject all acknowledgment of an emotional self, I had to reject all acknowledgment of Donna. I eventually lost Donna and became trapped in a new way. Carol strove for the unacceptable: social acceptance. In doing so, Carol took the stage. Willie, my other face to the world and the embodiment of total self-control, sat immobilized in the audience. Donna was still in the cupboard. When I was twenty-two, in search of myself, I again got into that cupboard and closed the door.

> *Staring into nothingness since time began,*
> *There and yet not there she stood.*
> *In a world of dreams, shadows, and fantasy,*
> *Nothing more complex than color and indiscernible sound.*
> *With the look of an angel no doubt,*
> *But also without the ability to love or*
> *Feel anything more complex than the sensation of cat's fur*
> *Against her face.*

Before Carol came along, I was sent to a special school.

I was three years old, in my prim and proper school uniform—blue checkered dress, navy blazer, always buttoned up to keep me in.

I loved the heavy oak doors of the school church, the polished floors, the colored glass up so high. I loved the way it all smelled and the trees that hung over into the playground. I loved cream buns at recess. I loved my metal school badge, which was sewn on to my blazer. Twenty-three years later, I still have it. I take it out from one of my many tins of treasures and bring back this school as though it were yesterday. Such treasures were the keys to myself, and God help anyone who touched them.

This was a private school with a reputation for good one-to-one attention and a policy of taking "special needs" children. Most of the children were older than I was. They were generally quieter and less invasive than other children.

It was thought that I was clever, yet I often didn't understand what was said to me. Although I was intelligent, I seemed to lack sense. Instead of talking with people, I would merely mimic them and talk endlessly over the top of their voices as though this sufficed for conversation.

I learned to enjoy doing things at the special school. The teacher would take us into the school church. A huge sheet of paper would be placed on the floor. Though I ignored them, there would be one child on either side of me, all working on the paper.

We each had a pencil and would draw until finally I would look up at the face that was joined to the hand that had drawn something into my picture. The teacher would try to make out figures from the huge half-scribbled masterpiece we had produced.

Sometimes, if I was interested in what the children in the classroom were making, I would be given some scraps so I could make my own artwork. Such things frustrated me. I didn't mind drawing but I hated trying to put things together to produce people and the like. I would spend my time making miniature worlds, full of bits of colored things and fluff and things that I might get under or climb over if I could somehow get myself into that tiny place. I'd put my face down at the level of my masterpiece, looking into it rather than at it, like a cat peering into a mouse-hole.

I never liked to sit on chairs. I had restless legs I couldn't keep still. I liked to feel the ground underneath me. The more of me that was on it, the better. But one day I got up onto the seat next to a big girl who was making a person out of a cardboard cone and paper. I was intrigued by her hair, which was pulled back into a long plait. I ran my hand down her plait. She looked around at me, and I was frightened by the way that her face was joined to her hair. I had wanted to touch her hair, not her. She told me that her name was Elizabeth. It was the first time that I could remember reaching out to touch someone gently, even if it was only her hair.

My mother would pick me up from the special school. I would always wave goodbye to the building. One day I waved goodbye to it for good. I'm told that a girl with cerebral palsy had hit me on the head with a rock. Perhaps she did. I was so oblivious to anything that didn't intrigue or disturb me that I didn't notice. It certainly didn't hurt my feelings, physical or otherwise.

By the time I had left this special school, I had begun to become Carol. Carol spoke to people. I learned to talk *at* people. People probably thought that the special school had done me some good. It probably had. It certainly did me no harm.

||||

I STARTED AT a regular primary school and took ballet classes at the same time. I had become very good at being told what to do, as this was what people liked, and people liked Carol. Being double-jointed, I could tie myself up into knots, which made people laugh, impressed them, and made my mother proud.

My mother had at last outdone her older sister. She had a dancing doll; her sister had only boys. My mother would twist and pull and damn near break my legs off, getting me to do the splits or bend over backward. My brother would enthusiastically hold one of my legs, and as I lay on the floor they would make my limbs into the hands of a human clock. Just like Carol, if they laughed, I laughed. They must have thought I was having a great time. Not only did they have a dancing doll; they now had a contortionist. What talent, what ability, what competition! I became the prized show-piece. Dance, little dancing doll. By the age of eleven, I was on painkillers for rheumatism, which I had developed in every joint of my body. I would grind my teeth and punch myself to kill the pain. It felt like my bones were scraping together. I stayed on painkillers for years. I only danced until I was seven, and I never did learn left from right.

||||

AT THIS PRIMARY school I learned to call myself mad. In my search for myself, when I was twenty-two, I returned to the house I had grown up in. The woman there showed me something she had discovered written on the wall of my grandfather's shack. I remembered when I had written it. It was after my grandfather died. I was about six. It read: "Donna is a nut." Strangely, it took me four more years to realize that normal children refer to themselves as "I."

Whether other children considered themselves my friends was irrelevant. My first chosen school friend was Sandra. I liked her smiling face, and she had dark, shining hair. She was a big girl and she was jolly. Other children teased her. She became, in her words, my "best buddy, old chum."

Other children played school, mothers and fathers, doctors and nurses. Other children skipped ropes and played with balls or swap-cards. I had swap-cards. I gave them away in order to make friends, before learning that I was supposed to swap them, not give them away.

Sandra and I would play the same game every day. She'd laugh, I'd laugh, we'd laugh. We'd sit side by side and scream in each other's ear. It made me laugh because it tickled, and I really didn't care what it was that she was screaming. She was the first person to play my games.

Through playtime and lunchtime Sandra and I would drink as much water as we could, until we felt we would burst. We'd choke ourselves until we turned blue, coughing and struggling to breathe. We would try to push our eyes in, in order to see colors, and we would scream and scream until our throats were red raw.

I thought this was great fun. I had discovered that I could share physical sensation. In the company of others my senses would cut off, and I would become so numb that, in order to experience something, I had to push myself to extreme limits.

Then Sandra found another friend. I called her fat; she called me mad. Together, she and her new friend tried to include me. I did not know how to cope with having two friends at once. I resolved the situation by rejecting them both.

I often played alone, swinging on the monkey bars, looking at my cards, climbing trees, pulling flowers apart, spinning around and around as I stared up into the sun. I would fall to the ground and watch the world spin. I was in love with life but I was terribly alone.

Other children were attracted to me. They would watch me in fascination, walking across the top of the monkey bars, swinging from a tree branch thirty feet up; in short, doing "mad" things.

Though we went to the same school, my brother had nothing to do with me. Where he had once been protective towards me, I was now a nut, a spastic, an embarrassment. I really do not blame him. Just as I lived in my own world, he was doing fine in "the real world."

Classes seemed to be an extension of the playground, and the playground seemed to be an extension of the classes. The teacher soon learned not to let me go to the toilet by myself, as I often wandered off and did not come back.

I'd be out in the playground enjoying myself. It seemed quite natural to me that if I did not like something I could find a way to avoid it. Looking back, I can imagine how strange it was for my teacher to be called out to the playground as one of her pupils was swinging and singing "On Top of the World" as I hung by my knees from the top of one of the school's highest trees.

On one occasion everyone had gathered down below me.

They shouted. I sang louder and louder and swung higher and higher. Finally I sensed their urgency and I got scared. Fearfully I climbed down. I still do not know if it was my actions that frightened me or the fear that someone might come up and get me. The teacher reassured me that I was not in trouble. Finally I came down. In dreams I replayed that day of defeat many times.

||||

AFTER ONE WEEK at primary school I was taken out of my class and, with four other children, placed in a special class called the "Country Infant Room." We had been selected from various classes, and while other classes changed rooms, pupils, and teachers each year, we were stuck with one another for the next three years. My teacher was a hard woman, perhaps for the same reason as my mother. She, too, was the mother of an unusual child.

The children in this class had special treatment, of sorts. Every so often some of us would go to Psych and Guidance. I remember very little of this. I remember the room, but the happenings obviously did not interest me.

||||

MY PROGRESS AT school was not too bad. I loved letters and learned them quickly. Fascinated by the way they fitted together into words, I learned those, too.

My reading was very good, but I had merely found a more socially acceptable way of listening to the sound of my own voice. Though I could read a story without difficulty, it was always the pictures from which I understood the content. Reading aloud, I would confidently continue, despite mispronouncing or inverting some of the letters or words. I would use different types of intonation to make the story sound interesting, though I was merely experimenting with my own voice, and my tone probably did not match the content of the story half the time.

My spelling was quite good. I had grasped phonetics well and had memorized the difficult words, so I appeared to be quite clever. My handwriting was poor and, despite practice, always remained behind the progress of the others year after year.

As for math, I would have done a lot better had my teacher given me numbers instead of colored rods. Each rod was a different color and length, and represented a different number. To me, they represented building blocks, and I would stubbornly insist on building towers with them, spiraling upward till only one of the smallest pieces would fit on top. Then I'd knock it down and start again.

Though I could add and subtract, I found fractions impossible. The concept of halves and quarters was lost on me. I finally found a way to understand them by some sort of translation via my understanding of subtraction. I may have found it hard to grasp complexities, but my attempts were nothing if not complex.

As for participation, I participated too much but never in the right ways. I chattered incessantly to myself, annoying everyone else. People said that I simply loved the sound of my own voice. They were probably right. I could sing, yet I would not sing with the others. I would mouth the words. Ten years later I would sing in the back row of my math class, but I never sang during music lessons.

||||

SHELLY WAS IN my class. Every year she'd have a birthday party, and every year her mother would charitably invite me.

Kathleen was in one of the other classes. Every year she'd tell me that I was either tenth or fourth on the replacement list for her birthday party. Every year I would get my hopes up. Every year Kathleen's friends would show up and she'd need no replacements.

Kay was from my neighborhood. She was probably the most popular girl in our class. She'd line up her friends and say: "You're my first best friend; you're my second best. . . ." I was twenty-second. A quiet Yugoslavian girl was last. I was pretty, I was cheerful and sometimes I was entertaining, but I did not know how to play *with* children. At most, I knew how to create very simple games or adventures and sometimes allowed others to participate, as long as it was totally on my terms.

||||

WHEN I WAS six my little brother was born.

Tom was unexpected, especially in view of the fact that it was thought that my mother could have no more children. Although I avoided looking at other people, I would look into Tom's baby eyes with no hesitation. I talked at him, did magic tricks to entertain him, and tried to teach him how to walk. I felt he was on my side and, given his behavior, perhaps I sensed something.

Tom was a headbanger. His only solace seemed to be banging his head against the wall. When he wasn't doing this, he was tearing around the house like a miniature tornado.

By the time Tom was two he could dismantle and demolish anything he laid his hands on at a speed that would put some adults to shame.

Tom liked the games we played, spinning around and around, then falling to the ground and watching the world spin. He loved jumping on every bed in the house with me. Sometimes we would lie down headfirst and come thumping down the stairs, the backs of our heads hitting every step until we crashed to the bottom. We would play with his blocks, separating all the letters into categories. And Tom loved jigsaw puzzles. He progressed so quickly through these that he was able to do adult ones by the time he was four.

Tom spoke freely from an early age, though he spoke with a strange pronunciation and accent and everyone was someone-or-other "boy." I was "Da boy"; even my father was

"Arkie boy." Though we were Australian, my little brother always sounded like a Scotsman who had just gotten off the boat.

When Tom was two, he was seen by a psychiatrist, who said Tom was the worst case of hyperactivity he had ever seen. I thought he was quite normal. Later, he was found to be sensitive to the colorings and flavorings in foods; allergic to yeast, and deficient in zinc. Tom and I were both given zinc. The child care center refused to keep him, as he was too much to handle.

Like me, Tom took to music like a maestro and, almost compulsively, could teach himself anything to perfection, though he could not be taught. I thank God for Tom; though he escaped a lot of the abuse and name-calling, he moved in my world.

||||

I WAS SEVEN when we moved to the big house. It was like a haunted house when we first moved in. (The previous occupant had died.)

At the new house Tom became haunted by two friends, which terrified him. There was "Mr. Leg" and the "Big Ans," which was later "The Big Hands." It seems I'd told him they lived up the stairs to my room. Although my little brother was my best friend, not even he had the right to trespass or touch anything in or near my room. Tom had to pass the stairs to go to the bathroom. His fear made this near impossible.

My mother turned this, her new prison, into a doll's house. I lived in the attic. After the first few weeks in that house, they put bars on the window. It seemed I was to become the loony who lived in the attic. I certainly acted like one. As I struggled year after year trying to join "the world" and finding myself compelled to withdraw into my own, I'd stand at the window, pushing my face into the bars and dropping objects "to freedom," distraught if they landed in the gutter, yet glad because no one would see them and know what I felt. That summed up my dilemma really; everything was a double bind.

||||

AROUND THIS TIME I was again tested for partial deafness, for although I could speak I often didn't use language in the same way as others and often got no meaning out of what was said to me. Although words are symbols, it would be misleading to say that I did not understand symbols. I had a whole system of relating that I considered "my language." It was other people who did not understand the symbolism I used, and there was no way I could or was going to tell them what I meant. I developed a language of my own. Everything I did, from holding two fingers together to scrunching up my toes, had a meaning, usually to do with reassuring myself that I was in control and no one could reach me, wherever the hell I was. Sometimes it had to do with telling people how I felt, but it was so subtle it was often unnoticed or simply taken to be some new quirk that "mad Donna" had thought up.

||||

WHEN I MET Trish she was behind bars, too. I had tried walking home from school down Martin Street, but the trees frightened me. They were the type that dropped all of their leaves and stuck out of the ground like huge knobbly hands with long, forbidding crooked fingers. Even without leaves, their character seemed to dominate the whole street so that it always seemed to be full of shadows. The footpath had strangely laid-out paving stones, so that it took a lot of concentration to make sure you did not step on any of the lines. I hated Martin Street.

I began to walk up Trish's street instead, and ended up doing so for years. There were houses with roses in Trish's street. There was always a trail of rose petals along the footpath after I'd walked home.

One day I stopped and looked at some children behind bars. They called me over. I asked why they were locked in. I did not seem to realize that they were simply in their grandmother's backyard, which just happened to be closed off by a tall, black cast-iron gate.

Trish had just moved to our school. She was a quiet, shy, and gentle girl with a very simple nature. She was also the eldest of three children.

Although I was always either indifferent or controlling, I felt secure in the belief that Trish was my older sister. We hung about together at school. I showed her how to rub her eyes and look into the sunlight to see colors. She shared her grandmother's marvelous homemade cakes and found someone she could talk to. Though I listened, I often did not hear, but I liked Trish, so I'd look straight at her and she did not seem to notice. I was her best friend, and she became my proof that I was capable of having one.

Mostly, we would ride bicycles, play in the park, play word games, and talk about the things we would like to have. I would sing and dance and play with my shadow. She would sit and watch me and laugh. I didn't mind. I liked Trish.

I went to stay at Trish's place for a couple of weeks. I had my little suitcase, and Trish had loaned me one of her teddy bears.

The first night there we laughed and giggled and made up funny names for things. Trish's mother told us to go to sleep. Trish cuddled her teddy, and I lay next to the one she had given me.

"I'm scared, Trish," I told her. "I don't want to go home but I don't want to stay here." She offered to let me sleep in her bed.

People had long since given up trying to cuddle me, but I wanted to be like Trish. I got into Trish's bed as though I were her. She cuddled me like her teddy bear. I was terrified. It seemed tears were welling up from a part of me long buried and forgotten.

We were two seven-year-old girls, one taking the comfort

of hugging for granted, the other rigidly tolerating it, finding it terrifying and excluding.

Trish's mother came into the room to check on the sleeping girls.

"What are you two both doing in the same bed? Come on, Donna, back to your own bed," she said.

"Good night," said a sleepy Trish.

"Good night," I echoed shakily.

For many years after that I had the habit of lifting the blankets and inviting in any strangers my sleeping ears had heard enter my room. I had become Trish.

I lay back in my own bed in Trish's room on that occasion, trying to be as neat as possible. I had begun by neatly rearranging the bed around my body, which I'd placed as perfectly in the middle as I could estimate. I had my arms over the covers, rigidly by my sides; a perfect picture of "neat."

I decided that I was taking up too much space in the bed. I moved myself over to the side of the bed and eventually got down into the tucked-in blankets, as though I were a piece of clothing that needed hanging up.

I was making too much mess. I got out of bed and sat on the side of it. I was taking up too much space. I sat on the tiniest edge of the end corner. I looked untidy in my nightie; I had to get dressed. I dressed myself for the next day, looking at the venetian blinds in the darkness, hoping the light would come soon.

The clothes I'd brought were not neat enough. I folded them all, trying to be as silent as possible, and repacked my case, placing it next to my legs, which dangled to the floor at the corner of the bed. I looked at Trish and wished that she was like me, and then I wished so much that I was like her. Tears rolled silently down my face as I watched her sleep. The room was silent. Inside I was screaming loud enough to wake the dead.

Trish's mother entered the room.

"Donna, is that you? What on earth are you doing? You silly girl. What's wrong? Come on, hop back into bed. Why were you sitting there?" she said.

"I don't want to go home," I said in a whisper.

"You don't have to," said Trish's mother.

"I don't want to stay here," I whispered.

"Where do you want to go?" said Trish's mother.

"I want to go," I repeated.

"You can't go, Donna; there is *nowhere* to go," she explained.

"Nowhere to go, nowhere to go, nowhere to go," I said over and over in my head, trying to understand the words, which my feelings obviously did not acknowledge.

Trish's mother helped me to get back into my nightie. I complied like a robot, hypnotized by my mind's repetition of the words "nowhere to go." If anything I'd ever heard summed up the nature of the trap I was in, those words captured it like Shakespeare.

Trish slowly disappeared from my awareness, but she became the cause of a dream that was to be repeated over and over for the next fifteen years. When I was twenty-two, I still woke up terrified and frozen, staring at the venetian blinds in my friend's room. Such simple things left such a long-term impact.

I had stayed away from home on many occasions by the time I was seven, but never had it affected me so emotionally. I'd been brutally exposed to my own vulnerability in a world I found foreign and unreachable. I became angry at my innocence and naïveté. Willie took the stage as the curtain went down on the first compromise I'd found between Donna and Carol: the dancing doll.

IIII

TERRY LIVED AROUND the corner. She was older than I was and she was Italian. I was eight. She was ten. I used to watch her. She used to watch me watching her.

I did not know how to make friends, so I would stand there calling this girl every four-letter word I knew. As my mother had a huge vocabulary of swearwords, I did this pretty well. Eventually this girl would take to her feet and chase me for several blocks. I'd always go away, and I'd be back the next day to do it again.

One day she caught me. She was about to "smash my face in" when she decided at least to ask me why I had tormented her so persistently for so long.

"I wanted to be your friend," I blurted out furiously.

"You're mad," she said with disgust. "Why didn't you just try to talk, like normal people?" I was silent.

Knowing what I know now, I would have answered: "Because I'm not 'normal people.'" We became best friends.

Terry was into smoking, learning new swearwords, and talking about boys, and was interested in my brother. I wanted somewhere to go, something to do, and to be free of the painful accusation that I had no friends.

She would take me to the Hogans' backyard. They owned a wood-yard, and we'd sit among the wood. I was eight years old. I coughed and choked and learned to smoke cigarettes as I learned to be Terry. Terry found me amusing; I was probably the cheekiest and rudest child she'd ever met. My little brother and I went about swearing at, questioning, and defying anything and everything.

Terry would go inside for lunch. I'd sit, legs dangling into the gutter, glaring defiantly at her house from across the road. I never felt as though I was missing out on lunch, because I rarely felt hunger. The only thing I was missing was inclusion, and when I wanted this I wanted it on my terms, so I could throw it away at some later date, as though friendship was an apple gone bad.

I was as obsessive about my friendship with Terry as I was about any friendship. They were always exclusive and excluding. If other children were included, I either took the stage or, most often, bowed out. Terry had become my entire world. We spent almost every available moment together, playing with her cats, collecting bits and pieces from garbage collections, taking trams and buses out to explore different suburbs.

Terry's mother liked me, and I was her daughter's excuse for getting out of doing housework or looking after the younger children. As I had echoed English, so I echoed Italian. Standing in the front yard of their house I'd cheekily parrot the commands this mother gave her children, with the mother's inflection and pronunciation.

||||

AT HOME THERE was a constant war raging around me. My father was living in the fast lane, and every step he took in independence was another footprint upon my mother's face. It got worse when my father's version of compromise was to set this fast lane on a collision course with the front door of our house, and the house became a hum of constant drunken parties and the ensuing brawls.

I had always accepted my mother's violence toward me. Somehow it did not seem to matter too much. After all, it was only my body. Perhaps in some perverse way these extremes were the only physical sensation I could feel *without* being hurt. Gentleness, kindness, and affection terrified me or, at the very least, made me very uncomfortable. My mother used to say: "If you really want to hurt someone, be nice to them." Perhaps she had learned that lesson from watching the way it often affected me. If this came from her own experience, God help her.

||||

I DECIDED TO go and live at Terry's house. I would wait until about one o'clock in the morning and then sneak out, leaving the door unlocked so that I could sneak back in by about six, before anyone woke up.

Around the corner at Terry's, I would creep quietly around the back, where I would throw stones at her bedroom window as she'd shown me, and she would let me in. I'd climb up into the top bunk with her and, secure with my chosen ten-year-old mother, I'd fall asleep. Waking up at dawn was no problem. Quite the contrary, I always woke up at that hour, and often still do.

One night Terry's mother was waiting to greet me at the back door. I was petrified. She looked terribly stern, and I thought she was going to send me home. Her daughter stood beside her looking guilty. From the Italian, her daughter translated: "My mother says that if you want to come around here to sleep you must come at a decent hour so that you will not wake the other children up." I was over the moon. I was so excited that I could not sleep. Heading out the door of my own place, I simply told my mother I would be going around the corner to sleep. Every few nights, however, I'd go back to my parents' house and lay rigidly in bed in my pretty prison in the attic and stare at the ceiling until my mind went to sleep.

||||

Shattered dreams, broken glass,
Echoes of a shattered past,
Too many names strewn about,
The kind that one can live without.
They're the shadows here, within,
That tear apart personality.

It is hard to say whether the violence of my family made me the way I was. What I do know is that I never replayed their violence over and over in my mind until I was much older.

Though I was very much a part of it, it is hard to tell whether I helped shape my family's situation or they helped to shape mine. As a child, the things that disturbed me, the events that shattered the security of my little world and caused me to play them over and over again in my mind, were events to do with the disturbing nature of that which others take for granted: kindness, understanding, and love.

I could comprehend the actions of another person, particularly if they were extreme, but I had trouble coping with "whole people"—their motivations and expectations, particularly to do with giving and receiving.

With violence, I knew where I stood. To call it the result

of "baser" emotions must be true, for I certainly found it easier to grasp. Niceness is far more subtle and confusing. Most children learn to welcome it and accept it. By the time I realized it was there, it came as a disruption that I was never quite prepared for. Possibly such preparation closes love out, but without it I'd panic and be in a state of shock. People would try to comfort me. Comforting either annoyed me or hurt me. I guess I was not "most children."

IIII

WHEN I WAS aware enough of the world around me to notice my father's violence, I found that it did hurt. My father hardly ever laid a hand on me, but I was very disturbed by the person I saw he could be.

The house seemed full of colors, and everything seemed to move too fast to make out, but I would always make all the right moves. I suppose it's like a person in a state of shock who does not remember how, but functions with great ability. Perhaps this is comparable to where I was most of the time.

More than anything, I was torn apart by the terror and hysterics of the person who could most get through to me: my little brother. Regardless of what else he'd do, the most disturbing thing was the noise and the sound of smashing glass.

Colors and things and people would fly, doors would get kicked in, and sometimes faces would, too. But it was never "whole people," only their pieces. The pretty things that got smashed seemed to be a greater tragedy than what was happening to the people.

Tom would scream. His face my mirror, I'd scream. No sound would come out. I'd pick up my little brother and get into the cupboard, my hands over his mouth, my arms closing out the sound from his ears. I'd feel his tears and his runny nose on my hands. My eyes were dry. He made me feel emotions and still had the decency to express them for me. More than anything else, my little brother frightened me by making me feel real.

Although there were similarities between us, Tom had only some of the difficulties I had. He had no trouble looking at people as long as he could maintain his attention span long enough. He had no aversion to touch, and although very interested in bright color and music, he wasn't obsessive about the surfaces of things, bright light, and tinkling sounds like I was. He didn't do the sort of things my older brother called "spastic," and although his language was poorly developed and unique, he addressed people directly for the few minutes or so he stayed attentive. At about three, he went from alternating between a permanent smile and a grimace to having a range of expressions. With this came his ability to form attachment.

I began to reject Tom. I had become his whole world. Whenever I left him, he would cling to my leg, crying: "No, Da. No, Da. Please don't go." I would keep walking, dragging him along like a sobbing deadweight. No matter what I said, he'd take it to heart. Perhaps it was the first time anyone had taken me seriously.

Tom began to sleep with the dog, a three-year-old boy curled up with his bottle on a flea-ridden rug, with a male Great Dane for a mother. It was as though I'd died. Two years later the dog went. It was as though Tom died at the same time.

||||

I DECIDED THAT I wanted to go to Terry's school. I had no friends at my own school and I felt Terry would always look after me. I refused to go to my usual school, and my mother had no choice but to send me along with Terry and the others if I was going to attend school at all.

The classroom atmosphere at Terry's school was chillingly cold. My teacher was a knobbly, snapping old goblin who got very angry with me and kept shouting that I was giving him ulcers. He would make me stand in the rubbish bin, and I would swear and he would throw pieces of chalk at me. The children in the class would laugh. This time I didn't.

Terry had her own group of friends and, being two years

older than I was, she had no intention of giving them up to hang around with "a child." I went around the school for weeks asking everyone I came across if they were my friend.

"But I don't know you," most replied.

"But if you did," I would persist, "would you be my friend?"

Eventually I gave up and sat in a corner of the school ground, against the back fence. After a few months two girls decided they would let me hang around with them. The things they talked about bored me. I drifted away from them mentally, and soon they, too, drifted away from me. I fell into a deep depression that lasted about a year.

IIII

I RETURNED TO my old school but hung about on the outside of any groups that tried to involve me. I stopped smiling and laughing, and the efforts to involve me only hurt me more, till I'd stand there with tears silently rolling down my face. At home I'd go up to my room and cry, saying over and over again: "I want to die."

Terry came around to the house sporadically, and sometimes I'd go around there, but I was becoming more and more distant and finding it harder and harder to relate.

I had begun to walk about the house like something returned from the dead—shoulders hunched, head bent, eyes fixed at my feet wherever I went. People would ask me what was wrong. I'd paint a smile across my face and try to impersonate my version of happy. "Nothing's wrong," I'd tell them in as short an answer as possible.

At this point I was as fragile as I'd ever been. If I had received a lot of love and attention at that point, I would probably have felt that it would kill me.

My mother tried, in the only way she knew. She bought me things. She began to bring me home potted plants. I would look at them and look at them and wonder: Why?

She brought me home a budgerigar she had got at the market pet shop. She told me that it was "spastic" and that it would not live long but she thought I might like to have it until it died. It certainly was deformed. Its wings seemed somehow back to front. It could not fly, but could only hop; and, like she said, it died after a few weeks. Appropriately I cried.

She brought me home the prettiest thing I thought I had ever had. It was a mother-of-pearl china dish with a matching lid, upon which sat an angel gazing into space.

She bought me a doll's pram. I ventured outside my room with it, dragging it repetitively up and down the stairs without much interest in what I was doing. I was acting normal, wasn't I?

My mother did not think so. Furious, she came storming up the stairs. I stood watching her, terrified. She picked up the lid to the colored china dish and smashed it on the floor. The angel lay scattered in pieces. My mother spat out words. I was to be locked in my room without anything but bread and water until she decided when I could come out. She left, slamming the door nearly off its hinges.

As if to prove the point, she returned with a jug of water and a glass. I lay facedown on my purple-colored bed in the violently purple-colored room and screamed into my pillow, drowning out all the noise around me. My mother left without closing the door.

||||

I KNEW THAT my father had come home. I had been listening to the noises downstairs. I figured that they were talking about me.

I knew my father would feel sorry for me. I picked up a piece of broken china from the floor and, through a misty wall of tears, cut lines into my face in anger at the injustice of what had happened. I slashed my cheeks, my forehead, and my chin. With nothing to lose, I calmly walked downstairs to make my silent statement. "Oh my God," said my mother, as though speaking some slow, deliberate line from a horror film, "she's fucking mad." The look on her face was one of complete shock rather than concern. I was, by this time, nine years old and very close to being sent to a mental hospital.

Inside my head, what I was doing was completely sane. I didn't know how to cry out for understanding. I was lost and trapped, and I was making a statement. I think my mother at least understood the severity of the situation; she gave up on the bread-and-water idea.

My father's eyes seemed to be crying out to reach me. It seemed he understood but, like me, either could not put it into words, was not "allowed" to, or realized that some things are better expressed without them.

IIII

I HAD A lot of cousins, and we often stayed at each other's house. I liked a few of them, but I hated Michelle. Nevertheless, Michelle wanted to stay over, and I made no objections.

Michelle and Terry got along like a house on fire. Not knowing how to cope with more than one person at a time, I told them I wanted to be on my own. They went off to play.

I never spoke to Terry again. She had been my only friend for over two years, and as she stood there, asking me "Why?" I stared back at her blankly as though she was playing some curious scene from a silent movie, the content of which was beyond my grasp. "I don't understand you," she said. "What did I do wrong?"

A few years later Terry ended up working in the shop down the road. When she spoke to me I still ignored her; when she looked at me I still looked away. "You're mad, you know that, Donna," she once said, trying to get a reaction. I looked up and glared viciously at her.

About a year later Terry's best friend was killed by a truck while crossing the road with her. Terry had watched her die. She came around to the house and told my mother as I stood nearby listening. She was reaching out for a desperately needed friend. I hadn't yet found out how to give second chances or try again. I ignored her.

Ten years after I'd first met Terry, as I was trying to piece my life together, I arrived on her doorstep. She greeted me and offered me her friendship as though my ten years of silence had made no difference, though she said: "You're the strangest person. I've never met anyone who ever did that. One day you were talking to me; the next day it was as though we'd never been friends." She never knew how much I sometimes needed her, or how important it was for me to close her out, and I never told her.

||||

I HAD BEGUN, long ago, to plan leaving home for good. I thought that I would live in the lane behind our house, where I would sleep in the long grass and live on the plums that hung over the fences. I still felt responsible for my little brother and I began to prepare him for when I left for good.

I began to tuck Tom into bed and tell him stories. The stories I told him, however, were not the fantasy stories children are usually told. I presented him with situations he might face and how he could close them out and avoid being affected by them.

I taught Tom about singing a tune over and over in his head, if what he was hearing hurt. I taught him about looking straight through people, even if you had to look into their eyes to convince them you were listening. I taught him about jumping up and down as he recited things in order to learn them, and I taught him about losing himself in the spots. We began with a dot on the wall and worked our way up.

Tom was probably relearning tactics he had already used. He certainly didn't find much of what I was teaching him very new. Still, he was learning how to cope. In the meantime, through teaching him, I was becoming more and more aware of my own type of behavior—why I did things and what I got out of them. I also told Tom that I'd be leaving home one day. He told my mother.

||||

FOR THE LAST few years my mother had not been as systematically violent as she had been before I started school. However, the more she realized that I intended to leave home, the more she tried to convince me, not of her understanding, but of her power over me.

My mother was also becoming aware that I was approaching puberty, which posed major problems for her ability to cope.

Every day she would either give me the graphic details about some horrible experience she had had with men, tell me how she had been robbed of a life by having children, or tell me there was no way I was going anywhere; she would keep me at home as long as she liked. Any defiance on my part, from the way I stood to the look in my eyes, was met with violence, intended to crush my will. What had happened to her little dancing doll?

||||

BY THE TIME I'd returned to my old school, I was so withdrawn that I had little idea of what was going on around me. As I gradually emerged, it was once again into a world of things. I became fascinated with words and books, and making outside order out of inner chaos.

There was only one thing that my mother and I would do together: play Scrabble. It was, I suppose, good for adding to my trivial collection of words; words that sounded nice, words that I loved to say over and over, words that belonged to brands of things. The brand names *became* their real names, not just the noun for what they were.

My mother used her understanding of words to read horrific murder novels, which she would get through like lightning. I used to read, too. I loved to read telephone books and street directories.

I eventually realized that I wasn't getting anything out of the novels I was being made to read at school. I could read them all fluently, but I was unable to pick up what the book was about. It was as though the meaning got lost in the jumble of trivial words. Like a person learns to speed-read, I would read only the main words in any sentence, and tried to let the feel of the book somehow wash over me. It worked to an extent. Instead of reading a book thoroughly and gaining nothing in terms of content, I was now able to scan one and be aware of the names of some of the characters and some of the things that happened to them.

It was as though, if I concentrated too hard, nothing would really sink in. Unless the task was something I had chosen, I would drift off, no matter how hard I tried to be alert. Anything I tried to learn, unless it was something I sought and taught myself, closed me out and became hard to comprehend, just like any other intrusion from "the world."

||||

I LOVED TO copy, create, and order things. I loved our set of encyclopedias. They had letters and numbers on the side, and I was always checking to make sure they were in order or putting them that way. I was making order out of chaos.

I loved collections of things and would bring home library books on the many different types of cats, birds, flowers, houses, works of art—in fact anything that belonged to one group. My projects at school were like this, too. If we were, for example, asked to write about cows, I'd produce a chart, complete with detailed drawings, specifying every type of cow. My interest may have been repetitive and lacking in creativity, but I was taking a renewed interest in my surroundings. This was a phrase I always compared with "waking from the dead." Such tiny steps were always great achievements.

||||

I HAD LEARNED how to make free telephone calls from the phone booth around the corner and would systematically go through the telephone book, phoning the first and last name listed under each letter. I would explain that I was phoning them because they were the first A, last B, and so on. Usually they would hang up; sometimes they would tell me off; but, like anything, once I started I had to finish. The important thing was that I had moved from focusing on things to communication with people. The telephone booth was my conveniently impersonal classroom.

Occasionally I would get some talkative old person on the phone and I would chatter away like a firecracker gone off and they could hardly get a word in edgewise.

I would also count the number of Browns listed in the phone book, or the number of variations on a particular name, or the rarity of others. I was exploring the concept of consistency.

I would walk about the house proudly spouting my latest discovery in the phone book. I could not understand why such things bored people stupid. I guess they had already grasped the concept.

My fascination for street directories took on a new dimension. I began to bring home stray cats and kittens, just as Carol had brought me to her house all those years ago. I began to name them after the street names I had liked in the index of the directory—Beckett after Beckett Street, Dandy after Dandy Street. It was important that I did this in alphabetical order, as though mirroring my own systematic self-development. I was moving forward from things to communication to attachment.

Though I could neither apply myself at school nor be told what to do, I was motivated, persistent, orderly, and systematic about that which might have held the attention of someone else for a few minutes at the most. It might have seemed that my world was upside down, but I needed consistency. The constant change of most things never seemed to give me any chance to prepare myself for them. Because of this I found pleasure and comfort in doing the same things over and over again.

||||

I ALWAYS LOVED the saying, "Stop the world, I want to get off." Perhaps I'd been caught up in the spots and the stars at a time when other children kept developing, and so I had been left behind. The stress of trying to catch up and keep up often became too much, and I found myself trying to slow everything down and take some time out. Something would always call me back.

Perhaps it wasn't that I lacked the feeling of hunger, or needing to go to the toilet, or needing to sleep. Perhaps my preoccupation with remaining a step away from full consciousness made it necessary for my mind to deny the awareness of these needs; certainly I would ignore the signs —feeling faint, anxious, or grumpy—always too busy to stop for such things.

Though the feeling that precipitated my "losing myself" was most often beyond my control, I found I could either give in to it or try to fight it. It was hypnotic, and I often found myself giving in to it and sometimes sought the feeling when it wasn't there. It was as though I was hooked on this state of being.

One of the ways of making things seem to slow down was to blink or to turn the lights on and off really fast. If you blinked really fast, people behaved like in old frame-by-frame movies; you got the effect of strobe lights without the control being taken out of your hands.

If anything, my blinking was sometimes a reaction to sound. If the tone of someone's voice disturbed me, off I would go. Similarly I would turn the sound up and down on the television, breaking up people's voices but happy to watch the picture, or intermittently block my ears off. This seemed to imitate the difficulty I sometimes had hearing people consistently.

I talked compulsively when I was nervous. I also talked to myself sometimes. One reason for this was that I felt so deaf when I said nothing. It was as though my senses only functioned consistently when I moved within my own world, and that meant closing others out. Years later, I had my hearing tested again. At the time, it was found that my hearing was better than average, and I was able to hear some frequencies that only animals normally hear. The problem with my hearing was obviously one of a fluctuation in the awareness of sound. It was as though awareness were a puppet, the strings of which were set firmly in the hands of emotional stress.

One sound, however, that I loved to hear was the sound of anything metallic. Unfortunately for my mother, our doorbell fell into this category, and I spent ages obsessively ringing the doorbell. After I had copped a bashing for this, they took out the batteries. However, an obsession is an obsession. I took the backing plate off the doorbell and continued to set it off manually from inside the door.

IIII

I HAD BEGUN to feel something was missing but I did not know what it was. I had a doll and wanted very much to cut it open to see if it had any feelings inside. I took a knife and tried to pry it open but became afraid of the consequences of breaking the doll and simply went on wondering for the next few years.

I was sure that I had feelings, but they did not seem to make the jump in my communication with others. I began to become increasingly frustrated, violent, and self-destructive. This was made worse by expectations for me to behave like a young lady. The world around me was becoming as unforgiving and intolerant as my mother.

I would talk and talk, regardless of whether any of my classmates was listening or not. The teacher would get louder, and so would I. She would send me to stand outside the classroom. I would go for a walk. She would tell me to stand in the corner. I would spit and shout: "No!" She would try to come near me. I would arm myself with a chair like some sort of wild animal. She would shout. I would bring the chair crashing down or throw it across the room. I was no young lady.

||||

AT HOME I'D begun to have night terrors. I would be sleep-walking and wake up in another part of the house, hiding from something in the room that only my sleeping mind had seen.

I once woke up after being bitten by a beautiful blue-eyed kitten that had suddenly turned into a rat as I went to pat it. I had, during the nightmare, gone downstairs and played the scene in the living room, before waking up as I switched on the light. I stood there screaming as the blood dripped from my hand; then, like magic, it disappeared and everything in the room changed back to how it was in reality.

Another night I woke up standing in the wardrobe doorway, rigid with horror, glaring at a doll that had suddenly returned to normal. Seconds before, I had seen it come to life, hands outstretched, its lips eerily mouthing words I could not hear, like some scene from a macabre horror film.

I had become literally terrified of falling asleep. I would wait until everyone was asleep and then, frightening as my mother had become, I would go into her room and stand there watching her sleep, feeling secure in the knowledge that if anything was to get me it would have to get her, too, and she knew how to fight. From sheer tiredness, I began to hallucinate. Images on the walls would move. Unknown to my mother, I lay stiff and silent under her bed, almost too afraid to breathe. Tears rolled down my face. I made no sound. Like at Trish's house four years earlier, I lay there in silence and waited for the light to come.

||||

IT WAS MY last year in primary school. I was twelve years old. It was the seventies, and my new teacher was something of a hippie. His face seemed to peep out from a bush of bristly hair. He was tall and gangly with a gentle voice that seemed somehow "predictable."

Mr. Reynolds was fairly "alternative," I suppose. He brought in records and asked us to tell him what we thought the music and songs were saying to us. What I liked, most of all, was that there were no wrong answers. Everything was supposed to be only whatever it was to each child.

We would put on plays, and everyone got to do bits of whatever they chose to do—setting up props, painting scenery, or trying different parts. Even the audience was made to feel that they had a role to play.

Mr. Reynolds never emphasized ability, but instead allowed me to show him what I was capable of, and he would tell me which things I did better than others. It was as though the class was his family and he had, for me, become my new father.

This teacher spent a lot of time with me, trying to understand how I felt and why I did the things I did. Even when he raised his voice, I could still sense his gentleness. He was the first teacher at that school to whom I had made an effort to explain what was happening at home, though I still never discussed what was happening within myself. His mood never changed. He never seemed to betray my trust.

It was the hardest school year I had had up until then. I already had quite a reputation as a weirdo, and after standing up for two other loners who were being attacked, I found myself in the line of fire.

||||

SARA WAS FROM England. She had the brightest red hair I had ever seen, and nobody could understand a word she said, which was nothing new to me. Sara's cousin would not play with her as she already had a best friend and probably did not want to be brought down by playing with someone the other children rejected.

At the same time a new boy joined our class. He was tall and scrawny, quiet, withdrawn, and looked a bit haunted. The other children began to call both of these children "Zombie." Neither had any fight in them, and I, able to identify with how it felt to be tormented, decided that I was going to be on their side.

The name-calling got out of hand. Perhaps such things had always been happening around me, but this was the first time I was aware of them. Other children in my class had begun to call me "Zombie," too, pushing my sanity to the limit as they chanted it over and over again.

I watched the other children get violent with these two children, pulling their hair, pushing, shoving, kicking, punching, all because they were different. I began to fight back at some of them, trying to kick people down stairs, hitting them with chairs, slamming fingers under desktops, and becoming hard, quiet, and brooding.

As the school year ended, my attendance had been poor, as had my concentration—as always. Mr. Reynolds told me, defeatedly, that he wondered if I had learned anything at all. He explained how important the final test was; it was to be the last test I would ever take at this school.

||||

THE PAPERS WERE put in front of us. My answers seemed to come from nowhere. I certainly had not studied for the test.

The test results were given out in alphabetical order a week later. Christine was thought to be the smartest girl in the class. She got a score of eighty-three. A boy named Frank, whose last name began with *A*, had the highest score read out so far, the prize for which was a scholarship to continue on to secondary school at an expensive private school. Mr. Reynolds got to the *W*'s and announced that he could not believe it. I bowed my head in shame, thinking that I had not done very well. Mr. Reynolds announced to the class that, contrary to all expectation, I had a score of ninety-four.

My score was two points lower than Frank's, but I had achieved the highest score for any girl in the school. Frank went to the private school. I went on to be a high school dropout three years later. In the meantime, Mr. Reynolds stood there, pleased as Punch. I had proved that, regardless of whatever else I was, I was not a "retard."

In the last week of school, Mr. Reynolds announced that he was getting married. Something snapped. I put my head into my desk and slammed the lid down on my head again and again and again.

The room had become a jumble. I was like a caged animal. I wanted to run. I ended up in the nurse's office, where Mr. Reynolds explained to me that his marriage did not mean we were losing him and that we were all invited to the wedding and a big end-of-year party at his house.

I went to the wedding. I sat proudly in the front row, oblivious to the remarks that this was where the relatives were meant to sit. I was on my best behavior. I sat on my own in that front row, said nothing, and waved to my teacher as he took his vows.

I went to the party. I hung in the background, too shy to take the stage, and otherwise having no idea what to say. I smiled and tried to look like I was having fun.

On my last day at the school, a friend and I were hanging about in the classroom while the other children were outside playing. We looked in the teacher's book, which Mr. Reynolds had left sitting on his desk. She read what he had written about her. I looked up my name under W, and a sentence jumped out at me from the page: "Donna Williams is a disturbed child."

Mr. Reynolds, who had been in the staff room next door, came in and caught us. He was angry.

"What do you think you are doing?" he demanded.

"Why did you write that about me?" I asked. "What do you mean I am disturbed?"

"You had no right to be looking in that book," he retorted.

The report had, it seemed, come from Psych and Guidance. I left that school torn between resenting him and being confused about the me he had been able to bring out.

||||

IT SEEMED THAT the older I got, the more obvious it became that I had trouble communicating, or perhaps I was just becoming more aware of people's often "concerned" remarks.

When I was in a talkative mood, I would often talk on and on about something that interested me. The older I got, the more interested I became in things and the longer I would go on about them. I really was not interested in discussing anything; nor did I expect answers or opinions from the other person, and I would often ignore them or talk over them if they interrupted. The only thing that was important to me was to talk in an effort to answer *my own* questions, which I often did.

If I did not know something, I would either pretend I did or convince myself that I did not care to know. If I had to ask questions, it was as though I did so to the air. It had been this way for as long as I could remember, and I used to become very frustrated, wanting to know something but finding it was more of an obstacle to address someone than the question was worth.

I developed various methods of getting around this problem. At school I would walk in front of someone to get their attention and then simply begin to speak on the subject I was concerned about, usually without letting them know why I was talking about something; that would have been too direct. People often ignored my chatter, thinking that I was making a series of statements rather than asking questions in the only way I could. This was complicated, I suppose, by the fact that I ignored or spoke over anything they said in response. Nevertheless, it was important for me to know that they were listening, so I began to open all of my sentences with "Hey" or "Y'know what?" and to end them with "you know?" "right?" or "okay?" These idiosyncrasies became so predictable that people would make fun of me, mockingly anticipating my usual beginnings and endings.

It was the same at home. My mother, knowing that it disturbed me, would sarcastically make me call her "Mum." Under threat of violence, I would comply, forcing the word out with such hatred that it sounded like I was swearing. Eventually I would, at most, call her by her first name.

Nevertheless, I wanted to know things. I wanted to accumulate knowledge. I would walk about talking, trying to attract attention and going on and on about something in a very indirect way. My mother called my means of verbal communication "wonking." This was equivalent in definition, I suppose, to "unintelligible, mindless babbling."

For me, this "wonking" was my way of conversing and was certainly not mindless. It took an incredible degree of courage to seek out an audience and talk about something I was interested in. To me, this made me painfully vulnerable. I was expressing something about my own personality and identity. The fear it inspired would simply not have allowed me to express anything personal in any other way.

It was as though I had even to trick my own mind by chattering in such a casual and blasé manner; any other way stopped at the point of motivation. It was as though I were emotionally constipated and the words could not otherwise escape my lips. If it were not for the methods I had devised, my words, like my screams and so many of my sobs, would have remained silent.

People would push me to get to the point. When what I had to say was negative, this was quite simple. Opinions that had nothing to do with my own identity or needs rolled off my tongue like wisecracks from a stand-up comedian.

I remember, when I was about seven, how I got a slap in the face after walking into someone's house and announcing, "It's very dirty in here," and following it up by enthusiastically informing the host that he "only had one arm." This was fairly typical of me, and I came to earn myself a reputation as rude, hurtful, and outspoken. Later this same quality sometimes came to earn me respect as someone who was "never afraid to say what she thinks."

Hiding behind the characters of Carol and Willie, I could say what I thought, but the problem was that I could not say what I felt. One solution was to become cold and clinical about topics I might feel something about. Everyone does this to an extent, in order to cover up what they feel, but I had actually to convince myself about things; it made me a shell of a person.

These were the same tactics I employed when I found it necessary to create Carol in order to communicate all those years ago. Deep down, Donna never learned to communicate. Anything that I felt in the present still had either to be denied or expressed in a form of conversation others called waffling, chattering, babbling, or "wonking." I called it "talking in poetry."

||||

I WAS TWELVE, and my mother and older brother had embarked on a new campaign of systematically teasing me. It began with them asking each other "What did she say?" at which the other would reply: "Don't listen to her; she's wonking again."

They had thought up a new name for me. I was now "a blonk." This meant that I was a moron. My older brother, secure in the knowledge that I dared not fight back against my mother's "pride and joy," would bring his face close up to mine, tilting his head from side to side as I did, and announce, "Wonk, wonk, blonk, blonk." His proximity deeply disturbed me, but now so did his words. Perhaps this was because he had invaded my personal space by putting his face so close to mine as he said this. Perhaps it was the way he mirrored my habit of tilting my head from one side to the other when I was trying to understand someone, or the fact that he had employed my tactics of creating "special" words.

Regardless of how, he had made me relate to what he had said; visibly the words had stung. My brother and mother, having got a reaction, hurtfully persisted as I viciously retorted with "I'm not mad!" till I finally gave up entirely.

My mother said that I had changed when I was twelve. Never before had I had to fight so strongly for the comforts of my own world. "The world" still seemed like either a battlefield or a stage, but I was forced to keep trying to "play the game," if for no other reason than to survive. I would have been happy to "let go" and retreat into my own world if not for my belief that my mother and older brother seemed to thrive on my strangeness and inability to cope. My hatred and my sense of injustice were my driving force to prove them wrong. At the same time, my fear of feeling kept calling me back into myself. Both drives were intense and had a shattering impact, both on the real "feeling me" within and the characters whom I threw at those who tried to reach me.

IIII

MY MOTHER HAD wanted to send me to a girls' school. I insisted that I wanted to go to a mixed school or nothing. I went to the mixed school.

The high school I went to was a rough school in a fairly tough suburb. Expectations at the school were not high, and I didn't disappoint them. I was disruptive, bad-mannered, and uncooperative. I fitted in well at first.

When I first started at the school, like many other first-year students I had no friends. It was not long before I attracted other loners. One by one I'd fight with them and inevitably end up in a brawl. I was earning quite a reputation as a fighter and a troublemaker, which were the main ingredients required to make one popular at this sort of school. Not only did I brawl with any friends I fell out with, I also brawled with anyone who picked on me or anyone else I felt was getting picked on.

Other rough kids thought I was wild and insane: swearing at the teachers, throwing things, walking out of school, and destroying almost anything I laid my hands on—including myself. I would try to get others to try to shake their hands off their wrists or shake their heads to hear their brains rattle. I would hold my breath and tense up my stomach muscles, exerting inner pressure on myself, until I turned red, shook, and fainted. The other students laughed and called me crazy. The teacher thought I was badly disturbed. I felt that I had not asked for "their world," I had no desire to participate in it and, if I had to, it would be on my terms; I was free either to walk out or to disappear whenever I felt like it.

||||

IN PARTICULAR, GYM class was bad news. I hated being in teams or taking sides or being told what to do. Any efforts to make me toe the line were met with thrown equipment, which could sometimes be dangerous. One teacher who was clearly ignorant of the depth of my problems once decided to "teach me a lesson."

This teacher made me stay back in the changing room alone with her and then ordered me to catch the cricket balls she threw at me viciously. I had always been afraid to catch; I had been hit in the stomach by the first one and then pelted as I ran away from the rest like the frightened little girl that I truly was. Her intolerance angered me, the throwing of the balls frightened me, but strangely her violence didn't hurt my feelings at the time. Looking back, it almost does.

||||

ART, POTTERY, AND woodwork were a Catch-22. I liked to make things but didn't like to be shown how, let alone be shown what to make or allow others to see it.

I liked music, but wouldn't sing; and even being there, given how much I liked music, made me vulnerable and caused me to misbehave in order to "break up" the class.

I learned to dislike math, as I had always done the working-out in my head but was now being told to "show the working-out." I simply took the answers out of the back of the book and transferred them onto the paper as a compromise.

In English, I would write, though never on the prescribed topic. I'd spend the time writing evasively about something that disturbed me. I'd write in such a way that it almost needed to be decoded to be understood, and I would always finish my work off with a lightly penciled sketch drawn over the writing, covering the length of the page, which, I felt, would more adequately capture what I was trying to express. The pictures, too, would often be no more than symbolic, as I could never reveal anything too personal unless I could create some sort of distance.

IIII

AWARE OF HOW little I was able to show my true self, I insisted that my name was not Donna anymore and that I was to be called Lee. This was to signify that people were not communicating with Donna, only with the characters that I felt they were worthy of: my anger, embodied in Willie, and my ability to perform and communicate, embodied in the emotionless and empty shell I secretly called Carol. Others were not even worthy of my explanation, which I have kept secret from everyone for twenty-three years.

Most of the children who knew me refused suddenly to call me Lee (which was based on my middle name) and I refused cheekily to acknowledge them. Eventually I developed several nicknames, most of which I would answer to. As long as they did not insult me by calling me a name I could not feel, I was happy to pay the price of answering to whatever other name they thought up.

At home I would still spend hours in front of the mirror, staring into my own eyes and whispering my name over and over, sometimes trying to call myself back, at other times becoming frightened at losing my sense of myself.

I was losing my ability to feel. My own world may have been a void, but losing my ability to keep a grip on it left me unmercifully in some sort of limbo without any feeling or comfort whatsoever. I, like so many other "disturbed" people, began to hurt myself in order to feel something. It seemed that other people's "normality" was the road to my insanity. My ability to close them out kept me sane.

Feed the stray cats, but don't bring home stray children.
Stray cats can take care of themselves.
Pretend they're not there, just pretend you don't care,
Leave stray children to somebody else.

As I was losing myself, my mother was coming to life. As I began to mature physically, she was rediscovering her own sexuality. My father stayed away a lot, and my mother had discovered that she could be a party animal. She began to get in touch with friends from her teenage years.

The house began to come alive to the sound of rock and roll, and the last thing my mother wanted was a pretty teenage daughter with behavior problems.

It seemed that there was no excuse. As soon as I walked in the door, home from school, I would be met with punches and kicks, hair-pulling and harsh words of filth. As always, I'd never scream.

I had a friend from school, whose family, like mine, was in pieces. Sometimes I would go to stay at her house, sometimes I would be sent. Sometimes I would not be allowed to stay, and my friend would try to sneak me in. One night I had to find a place to sleep for myself.

Another girl from school lived a few blocks away. I had gone straight around to her house when I found I had no place to stay. I hardly knew her, but she had taken one of the stray kittens that I'd brought home and had been forced to find another home for before it got killed by my mother. I interrupted this girl's evening meal to ask her if she could arrange to let me into her garage to sleep.

It was set. I went to this girl's house at about nine P.M. I had been walking around and around and around the street blocks in her neighborhood to pass the time. But the garage was locked and all the lights were out.

I found an alleyway and, secure in the duffel coat I wore everywhere, lay down and tried to sleep. I heard the sound of footsteps and, like lightning, took to my feet and bolted. It was probably the motorcycle policeman who had been following me as I walked around the streets.

I considered sleeping in an abandoned house across the road from my friend's house. But people had said it was haunted, and I was too frightened to stay there.

I sat on my friend's neighbor's fence. It was two o'clock in the morning. It was summer in Australia, and people often found it hard to sleep, including twelve-year-old girls in duffel coats.

A woman walked across the lawn in the darkness toward me. I got up to run. "It's okay," she called. "I just want to talk to you." She seemed so terribly calm and invited me inside for a cup of tea. In my mind, it was the fantasy I had been awaiting for almost ten years; she was an imaginary version of Carol's mother.

"It's two o'clock in the morning," she said casually. "Would you like some cereal?" I accepted without a thank-you. "Would you like to call your mother and let her know where you are?" she asked.

"She knows where I am," I replied.

"How could she know you're here?" asked the lady.

"She thinks I am next door," I replied. "My friend lives next door."

"Then, why aren't you there?" she inquired.

"Didn't want me to stay," I said.

The lady said I was welcome to stay and showed me to a tiny little green room with a tilted ceiling and a mirror on the wall. I could have stayed forever. Embarrassed, I left the next morning and never saw her again.

||||

EVERY DAY I walked home from school through the cemetery. This day I had decided that I was not going to cry anymore when I got home. I would go through the door this time and I would look straight into my mother's eyes and smile.

The greeting was the same. This time my hair, enmeshed with her fingers, was being torn out. Time and again, my head met the wall with a thump. I felt the stickiness of my own blood and hair upon my forehead. The hallway was becoming dark. I looked straight up into my mother's eyes, a painted smile stretched across my face.

A voice was pleading: "Please, leave her alone."

My mother's voice defeatedly commanded: "Why don't you just fucking cry?"

My energy was gone. I melted to the floor.

I woke up and stared at the ceiling of my bedroom. The silence inside my head was incredibly loud. People came and went, ashamed. No doctors came. Donna was back. She stared vacantly at the ceiling. Screaming, shouting, people were afraid now. Donna did not respond. My older brother, knocking on my forehead as though it were a door, demanded, "Anybody home in there?" I didn't care at all, nobody was going to answer the door. His face in my face, up to his old tricks. "Leave her alone," said a voice.

At the table, I was looking at a plate of colors, a knife and fork in my hands. I looked through the plate of colors, and everything faded out. Hands disturbed my vision—a silver knife, a silver fork, cutting up a color.

There was a piece of something sitting at the end of the silver fork. It sat there very still. My eyes followed the piece from the fork to a hand. Frightened, I let my eyes follow the hand to an arm, which joined a trunk, a head, a face. My gaze fell upon the eyes, which looked back at me with such desperation. It was my father. I retraced his arm, his hand, the fork, the piece of color, then back again. Silently tears streamed down my face. It was my grandfather all over again. I was back to two years old, and my grandfather was feeding me. I ate from the fork.

||||

IT WAS DECIDED that I should stay in the country for a while. The three-hour trip up was in slow motion. Everything was back in bits. Everything was a captivating pattern of colors —green triangles, gold squares, a blue into which I looked up and felt myself swimming.

I entered the country house, eyes glued to the floor. It was like when I was three; carpet seemed to go everywhere, stretching like a series of long snakes. There was a little girl in a high chair who caught my attention. Taking in only her size and shape, I thought, Good, my little brother is here, too.

There was so much silence in my own head, and everything else seemed so "external." It all seemed a thousand miles away.

I walked; crunching sounds, happening beneath my feet, as I walked a long line. I climbed; dirt and grass, my old friends, beneath my hands and feet. I swung up and down on a swing, head back, higher and higher. That's it; I'm going to fly.

A girl began to watch me. Her voice, so far away, I followed automatically. My hand upon short, light brown hair. It moved away of its own accord. Startled, I saw it was a horse.

The little girl in the high chair chattered. Her voice was light and playful. I tried to understand. I came close up to her, listening to the sound. We began to talk to one another.

Interrupted. An adult moving about. An oven opening. Cooking? "Yes, it's eel. Have you ever had eel, Donna?" My name struck me like a slap in the face. I went into the living room, sat on the couch, and listened to music. The room full of colors, music in my head.

I had some money. I liked the lady in the house; I was going to buy her something. Stones crunching beneath my feet. My hand clenched around money. Hand open, hand closed, hand open. Look at the coins! I could hear my own voice inside my head giving me a running commentary and, in doing so, calling me into awareness. "What am I doing? What am I doing? What am I doing?" All the sentences were becoming patterns of sound again. Was I talking? Did anyone see my lips move? Did any noise come out?

I began to fall in love with life. I loved the sky. I loved the ground. I loved the trees, the grass, the flowers. I loved the glass windows; I waved hello to myself. I could tug at my hair and feel something. I began to chew on my arm, tasting the salt on my skin, and looking at my freckles. I was me. I loved the silver legs of the high chair and the laminated bench-tops; I'd put my face on them and even lick them. I loved the floor and the roof and the doors. I loved the little girl who talked to me and her mother who had fed me eel.

My mother came to pick me up. On the way back to our house, I watched everything leave. I watched the trees leave and the golden fields. I watched the road stretch on and on and on.

IIII

BACK IN MY old attic room I spent all my time losing myself in the pattern of the wallpaper. I'd sit there even as night fell, silently staring into the darkness. When I needed to go to the toilet I'd get up and take a few steps across the floor before going on the purple carpet I hated so much.

As time went by I became more and more aware of myself through doing this. I'd watch a puddle form and giggle as it seeped into the precious carpet. Symbolically this was "my world" with a "me" in it. The more I covered that carpet, the more of a "me" in the world there was. The smell didn't worry me. The smell belonged to me and closed out other things. By the time my mother discovered what I'd done, my purpose for doing this had already been achieved. I'd called myself back out of my body into my room—a room I'd made sure belonged to me.

One day my mother picked up the rug that covered the latest puddle. Complete shock registered on her face and matched my own nauseating fear that my world would be taken away for having been found. Incredibly she left the room silently.

She returned to drag me off to the doctor. She went in, and I sat in the waiting room. She returned, drove to the hardware store, and bought a plastic potty. "You'll go in this," she ordered. My older brother mocked and teased me. Amazingly she told him to stop. No one was to talk of it, not then or ever.

They discussed what to do with the carpet that had for the

last few months been my urinal. "Let her put up with it" was the first solution. It must have dawned on them that I wasn't too disturbed by that. They tore it up, and I had bare floorboards to dance and roller-skate on. The carpet and the behavior had gone. I never used the plastic potty; I went back to holding on and keeping control.

||||

I WAS BORED. I wanted to go to school. It seemed that I had not attended school for six months and things were not going to be that easy. My mother fabricated a story. I was to learn that story and learn to tell it.

My mother sent me into the principal's office with a note of explanation. It seemed that I was to be the daughter of a single mother who could not be contacted as she worked every day to try to support my three-year-old brother and me.

It seemed that we lived in a flat in the suburb next to the school and I had the sole responsibility of looking after my little brother. I had recently arrived, so it seemed, from a school in another state, which was going to send them my details. I had apparently done well at this school.

The real story was that I lived in a house three suburbs away, I had two brothers, the younger of whom was now nine years old, and we lived off whatever money my mother could get out of my father. I had been attending the local school three suburbs away in the same state, but I had not attended for the last six months. I had done very badly at this last school.

||||

EVERY MORNING I had to catch a bus and tram for the long journey to this new school. It certainly was a new school. There were shiny red banisters and curved tinted windows. There were indoor carpeted staircases everywhere, and the whole place was a mass of corridors; a puzzle in which you had to choose the right decor.

I liked the banisters, which led to hallways with red doors running off them. I was constantly going into strange classrooms and sitting down before being escorted out and pointed in the direction of my own class.

I was quiet and eerie. I never understood what I was being asked to do, so, sitting obediently in the classroom, I would draw pictures, before tearing them into tiny pieces and creating piles with them on my desk. The teachers were fairly patient with me—or, at least, I cannot remember that they interrupted me. Perhaps they left me alone, like a new student who needed time to settle in. Perhaps they were simply glad that I was not disruptive. Perhaps they thought that I was backward.

On lunch breaks, I would wander through the school, watching the various colors that disappeared under my feet, and I would stop sometimes and stare at something for the entire break, like the polished floor of the gym or the reflection in the curved tinted-glass windows. Other children disgustedly began to comment that I was mad. I ignored them, choosing not even to look at them or even let it register that I'd heard. I'd heard it all before.

Another girl was said to smell. Nobody wanted to know her. She lived in the council flats with her drunken father and had the responsibility of looking after her three younger sisters. I guess she thought I could relate to her. Her father was hard and violent and used to hit her. I could relate to that.

She was tough and a fighter. I had, it seemed, lost all of my fight. She began to fight people who teased me. I never rejected her, and she hung around, helping me find my way to classes, hopelessly trying again and again to teach me to read the timetables. For once I was allowing other people to do all the talking. If I replied at all, it was either with "H'm" or in very short sentences.

I began to participate in art class. I had a huge sheet of white paper upon an easel and I painted a series of colored fluffy spots. Somebody asked what it was. "Don't know," I replied. I decided, after that, that I would only draw in black and white; black on a white background.

I began to draw stars everywhere and on everything. My mind was clearly back to when I was a baby, though I now had the ability to lash out violently if anyone tried to get too near to me. One day someone at the school did. I have no idea what they may have done or said, but they had tried to get too near. I picked up a chair and began to swing it. I was asked to leave the school. I had lasted two weeks.

||||

I ARRIVED AT a new school one more suburb away. This was to be my last chance. If I had trouble at this new school, I would be sent to a children's home. I was fourteen years old.

I tried to be as cooperative as possible, which meant that, instead of lashing out at others so much, I would take it out on myself.

I had been put on painkillers for rheumatism, to be taken only when I needed them. The pain by now had become excruciating, and I would slam myself side-on into the walls and knock my head against them in an effort to ease the pain.

Painkillers hardly seemed to help at all, and I felt as though my bones were grinding together in the same way that I would grind my teeth. I had also been put on "nerve tablets" by the local doctor, to calm me down. The doctor on the other corner of the street had given me sleeping tablets, as I was still terrified of sleeping. Instead of taking any of these, I would store them up and take a handful of them at a time when I had put up with more than I could take; then I'd eventually find a place to sit, propped against a fence somewhere on my own, and everything would disappear.

As before, I would swing between silent and vegetative, wild and destructive, and just plain weird. As I continued to slip back into myself, I began to be quietly escorted out of class and sent to welfare officers and shrinks, where I would sit and be observed as their words went on and on, falling on my deaf ears in some sort of annoying pattern of sounds.

All I ever remembered of such sessions was the beginning: "Come in, Donna; we would like you to meet . . ." It was just like my records when I was little: "This is an original little long-playing record. . . . We are going to begin now to read the story. . . . You can read along with me in your book. . . . You will know it is time to turn the page when Tinker Bell rings her little bell like this. . . . Let's begin now. . . ." I don't think I was mad, but I was certainly very distant and too far away to be reached.

||||

I WAS BEING myself. I had been sitting in class losing awareness of everything around me as I stared into nothingness. It was a reading class, and I had my pen in my hand and had been staring straight ahead in the direction of a piece of green chalk on the blackboard ledge.

My folder, the cover of which I had torn to shreds, had now been painted by me in shiny household paint. My hand was moving mechanically back and forth as I stared straight ahead.

The teacher's voice had a tone of sympathy, and I panicked momentarily, thinking that I must have been sick.

As I was lifted from my chair, I grabbed for my folder and found that it had been carved almost in half and was covered in a mess of blue ink, as was my hand. My pen was merely a tube of clear plastic with the nib hanging limply on the end of it and blue ink everywhere.

I was escorted to the assistant headmaster's office and placed in a chair. "What's your name?" said an interrogating voice. "Where do you live?" Mechanically I replied, stating my name and the address I'd been taught to give. "What's your name? Where do you live? What's your name? Where do you live? What's your name? Where do you live?" came the echoing assault upon my ears. I replied, in turn, to each echo, becoming faster and faster, building up to a crescendo before jumping to my feet, grabbing the chair that I was sitting on and screaming: "I'm not fucking mad!"

"It's all right Donna," came a voice. "Would you like to come with me?" it said calmly. I was led away to an office and given some paper to draw on.

I was being treated well at this school. They had stopped keeping me in or giving me lines. It was simple. If I misbehaved beyond the level of tolerability, I was escorted out to sit in the office again, under observation, and if I liked I could draw.

IIII

I LIKED GOING to art class. I began to play as though the whole room were my toy chest.

In a dream state, I jumped from desktop to desktop, a chair raised above my head, which I shook from side to side as though it were a pair of maracas as I sang, first slowly and then fast, the song "I Go to Rio." I was putting myself, my words, steps, and actions, on speed 33 and then speed 78. The rest of the class was in stitches. They would watch me, enthralled. I really didn't care. It was as though they were in another world, looking at me having fun in my world under glass.

Stella was one of the children watching. She was Italian, with bleached, cropped hair like cotton wool, and cartoon-like features. She had had a lot of behavior problems and had no hesitation in joining me. We did a duet around the room. Like a sellout concert, the other students went wild watching, and we became friends. This girl was intrigued by my "madness." She admired the way that I didn't seem to care what anyone thought of me and the way I stood up for myself when people tried to stop me. I also became her yardstick and an excuse for her own bad behavior. Truth be known, she led me into more mischief and danger than I would have been likely to get into on my own.

I also made my own classes. Often I found myself wandering out of the school.

Each experience would lead to another. Sometimes Stella would come with me. I was never going anywhere in particular, just going. I'd climb the stairs at the high-rise flats, play in the elevator, or try to find how to get on the roof with every intention to jump off and "fly." Other times I'd walk into factories and explore the materials around and sometimes ask people what they were making. I played in car washes, walked along endless railway tracks, rode on the back of trams, and joined classes at other schools. When I was approached or challenged, I'd bolt. I think I learned a lot about things this way.

My teachers in the meantime were often out looking for me—sometimes even driving around the streets to catch me and bring me back. I wasn't misbehaving, however; if they'd found me and told me where to go, I'd have followed.

IIII

AT HOME I became quiet, brooding, and intense. I would walk up to the faces of family members, lunge forward and weave my hands back and forth in repetitive figure eights. *Slap!* came the response again and again, and I smiled with every hit. I worked especially hard on my mother. I tried to assert how completely in control I was. She tried to prove that someone like her could never have a "spastic" for a daughter. Eventually it was clear she was willing to play for the ultimate stakes. I decided my obsession wasn't worth the price.

I was living as completely as I could within my own mind, and what I did express I expressed in a very symbolic and disturbing manner. I decided to murder a part of myself. As anger grew, this internalized version of my mother threatened to shut me out from my inner self. I decided to kill Willie.

I had been given a small boy doll dressed in jeans and a shirt. I wound a scrap of red tartan around its body, which was the material my grandmother had often worn. I colored his eyes with green crayon so that they glowed an iridescent bright green.

I found a small cardboard box and painted it black. I

waited until no one was at home, then went outside to the fish pond and buried my symbolic version of Willie in his black coffin, going to great lengths to cover up any sign of the burial. I went inside and wrote him an epitaph: *Let go, I say, my tear-soaked stranger. . . . I'm afraid that you have drowned beneath the many dreams which did evade you and the many stars so out of reach. Let go, I say. I must take over . . . and perish in a past of shadows, so that I may walk a stronger path.*

Looking back, it was not a return to my nothingness that I sought. This incident was an expression of my desire to overcome the conflicts within that had made my world of nothingness so necessary. The conflict was caused, and always had been, by the necessity to give up control and interact with others. The more I tried, the worse became the conflict. The more I kept to myself, or kept others at a distance, the clearer things became.

||||

As ALWAYS, MY motivation to interact was to prove my sanity and avoid getting locked up in an institution. My inability to maintain this situation for any length of time was due to the state of mind of which "my world" consisted. In this hypnotic state, I could grasp the depth of the simplest of things; everything was reduced to colors, rhythms, and sensations. This state of mind held a comfort for me that I could find nowhere else to the same degree.

People often asked me what drugs I was taking. Ever since I was a toddler my pupils had been huge and often made me actually look like I was on drugs. When I did take prescription drugs, it was more to provide me with an excuse for my behavior or to intensify my already distant state of awareness. This state of mind was, I suppose, like some sort of semiconsciousness, as though my body was awake but I was still asleep. When I gave up being aware of and responding to things around me, I would return to this state and would only then feel I was being true to my nature. When I stayed aware and alert to what was happening around me, it took a lot of energy and always felt like a battle. I suppose it appeared that way to others, too.

If I was like this because of brain damage, it did not affect my intelligence, although it seemed that I lacked what is called "common sense."

Anything I took in had to be deciphered as though it had to pass through some sort of complicated checkpoint procedure. Sometimes people would have to repeat a particular sentence several times for me, as I would hear it in bits, and the way in which my mind had segmented their sentence into words left me with a strange and sometimes unintelligible message. It was a bit like when someone plays around with the volume switch on the TV.

Similarly my response to what people said to me would often be delayed as my mind had to take time to sort out what they had said. The more stress I was under, the worse it became.

The significance of what people said to me, when it sank in as more than just words, was always taken to apply only to that particular moment or situation. Thus, when I once received a serious lecture about writing graffiti on Parliament House during a class trip, I agreed that I'd never do this again and then, ten minutes later, was caught outside writing different graffiti on the school wall. To me, I was not ignoring what I had been told, nor was I trying to be funny; I had not done *exactly* the same thing as I had done before.

My behavior puzzled others, but theirs puzzled me, too. It was not so much that I had no regard for their rules as that I couldn't keep up with the many rules for each specific situation. I could put things into categories, but this type of generalizing was very hard to grasp.

Everything over which I did not have complete control (that which occurred through the motivation of others) always took me by surprise, often either shocking or confusing me. It often felt like the effect one gets in a 3-D movie where you duck and weave as everything seems to be coming at you. For me, life was a movie theater and my only means of walking out was to close out anything else that was going to reach out and affect me, particularly touch or affection. Just like in a 3-D cinema, the things on the screen began to invade my world. That which was only a picture came to life.

This was the frightening reality of moving within "the world"; and, in comparison, mine held a lot more comfort. "My world" may have been lonely but it was predictable and came with guarantees.

I don't feel that I was like this because of my home life, although that was certainly not "normal." I believe that I was like this because of a constantly changing state of awareness. My home life only affected some of the forms that my behavior took, though not the behavior itself. I didn't close out the world because of the violence so much as the violence was closed out because it was one of many parts of "the world."

||||

I HAD MADE friends with a girl named Robyn. She was a new kid at school and didn't have any friends yet. I went home with her to her house, which was a council flat not far from the school. We sat outside beneath a tree and called it "our tree." We sang and danced like a pair of overgrown fairies in the grasslands in the center of the council estate. She liked being made part of my world, and more important, she didn't try to invite anyone else to join in.

Sitting beneath this tree, this first day, it began to get darker. I saw a man approach us who simply stood at a distance and waved.

"What's he waving at?" I asked her.

"Who?" she replied.

"That guy there, the old guy," I explained.

She could see no one, and asked what he looked like. I explained, describing his size and build, his stance, looks, and dress.

"That sounds like my grandfather," she said in surprise.

We went upstairs and she told her mother about what I

had seen. I described the man again, and her mother agreed that it certainly did sound like my friend's grandfather. Three days later her grandfather died.

At school strange things were happening. I would have daydreams in which I was watching children I knew. I would see them doing the most trivial of things: peeling potatoes over the sink, getting themselves a peanut butter sandwich before going to bed. Such daydreams were like films in which I'd see a sequence of everyday events that really didn't relate in any way to myself. I began to test the truth of these daydreams, approaching the friends I'd seen in them and asking them to give me a step-by-step detailed picture of what they were doing at the time I had the daydream.

Amazingly, to the finest detail, I would find I had been right. This was nothing I had controlled, it simply came into my head, but it frightened me.

||||

My ability to "know" things fascinated my friend Robyn's mother, and I became welcome to stay at their place, which eventually became my second home.

The first night I stayed for tea, Robyn's mother was appalled. "What on earth do you think you're doing?" she exclaimed as I scooped up my mashed potatoes with my fingers and put them in my mouth. "You'll eat with a knife and fork, Missie," she said sternly. I began to scoop up my food, holding my fork like a shovel. My friend's mother took my plate away, saying: "You'll learn to eat properly or you won't eat at all."

Although my mother had given me detailed eating, smiling, standing, and manner lessons, they had generally been short-lived, so I, like my two brothers, had always been allowed to eat like this. None of us was ever taken out anywhere (my mother hated going out to public places), so it didn't seem to matter. Nevertheless, this woman was not going to be defeated and told me that, if I learned to eat properly, she would take both me and her daughter out to a restaurant. I learned to copy them like a prize actress.

One thing that I couldn't learn was how to feel. Robyn's mum would always hug her before she went off to school, and she insisted on doing this to me, too.

"Come and get a hug," she said one morning after I'd stayed the night there.

"I don't like to," I said.

"You're going to have to learn to," my friend's mum insisted. "If you're going to stay here, you will learn to do what my own daughter does."

So every morning, like a rock, I learned to tolerate being hugged. I told my friend's mother that being hugged hurt me and that it felt like I was being burned. She insisted that this was nonsense, but that didn't help the feeling go away.

At first my head would spin. I felt that I was going to faint. I would only hug her when routine called for it; and in exchange I became her "foster" daughter, with the packed school lunches, the clothes, the collection of school report cards, and eventually even a bed of my own.

At first I had to share a bed with Robyn. This was impossible, as I could hardly sleep while I was trying to maintain the distance between us. Nevertheless, I felt quite close to my friend and began to tell her about some of my problems.

> They'd save scraps for the stray cats,
> And leave out the plate.
> It'd always be empty the next day.
> What she didn't finish, she'd leave for the cats,
> For she knew what it felt like to live like a stray.

I always paid for closeness with fear and found that, although I did not want to go home, I sometimes could not bear my growing emotional dependence on Robyn and her mother. Instead I would go across to the other side of their suburb, hang about until the last tram had left and then walk back in the dark to where my friend Stella lived. I became her alibi and her scapegoat.

Stella's mother said that I was evil and thought that I was a bad influence on her daughter. Her daughter no doubt encouraged this impression by blaming my supposed example whenever she got caught for doing anything. Nevertheless, the daughter liked me and was always happy to be involved in any new drama.

Stella lived in a little terrace house, at the back of which was a cobblestone alleyway. I arranged with her to climb her back fence and sleep in the tiny shack in the back of her yard.

In the early hours of the morning I would climb this tall corrugated-iron fence, scramble over the roof of the shack, and let myself in. I'd snuggle in, next to her brother's greasy motorcycle and, wrapped securely in the duffel coat that had become my mobile home, I'd fall asleep. Her parents kept bottles of homemade wine in this shack, and sometimes, if I was cold, I'd smash the top off one of the bottles and fall asleep drunk. In the morning my friend would sometimes sneak out with the scraps from the evening meal, which I was always grateful to get.

I was beginning to look quite rough. I never washed my coat and rarely took it off. If I did, I would place it beside me and take it with me if I left the room. My hair was often greasy, and I never brushed my teeth. I began to wash myself under the taps in the front yards of people's houses.

My friend Robyn understood. I had explained to her my need to "disappear," and I was always welcome to stay whenever I wanted to. Her mother made a point of talking to me about the way I dressed and spoke, and tried to teach me class and sophistication. I liked her, and I was a good student. I stopped swearing and began to behave more like a "lady"—at least, while I was there. The duffel coat still followed me everywhere and did for another eight years.

Robyn's mother had taken on a huge project when she took me in; but away from her house not a lot had changed.

I may have been secretive and private but I was not sly or cunning. Her rules, like all rules, only applied to the particular situation I learned them in.

I certainly believed in the value of the things she had tried to teach me, but everything I learned I learned for her. I simply never realized that such lessons had relevance for *me*. Thus, no sooner was I out of the door than my manners, stance, and means of communicating went back to square one.

There were, however, a few exceptions. Most important, Robyn's mother was the only adult I would listen to about anything to do with my own body. She also taught me how to tolerate affection, proximity, and concern. I learned to trust Robyn enough to let her brush my hair and tickle my feet and forearms, and this allowed me to experience the pleasure and relaxation I could get from touch albeit in a very primitive form.

The experiences I had gained from this family unit also helped me several years later when I learned to reflect on what I had learned as a means of mechanically constructing a more stable, presentable, and sociable identity under the committed guidance of an equally invaluable human being: my psychiatrist.

Every so often I would go home. My mother had recently rented a piano, and I loved the sound of anything that tinkled, and had since I was very small. I would string safety pins together and, when I wasn't chewing on them, would tinkle them in my ear. Similarly I loved the sound of metal striking metal, and my two most favorite objects were a piece of cut crystal and a tuning fork, which I carried with me for years. When all else failed, music could always make me feel.

I believe that I had always played music, even before I ever had the use of an instrument. I would create tunes in my head, and my fingers would play the intervals.

My mother also had a passion for classical music and had decided to teach herself to play.

As soon as I had noticed it, I was at the piano in a flash. Within a few minutes I was tapping out tunes I knew, and a little later I began to make up tunes, playing them quite fluently. It had occurred to me at the time that this is what I had been doing with my fingers when I had heard music in my head.

My mother had decided to hang about and watch me in her usual critical way. She sat down and showed me how she had learned to play some pieces in a beginner's book she had bought herself. She began to play, slowly, with two hands. I watched her and looked at the music. She explained how some of the notes went up and some of the notes went down and that the distance between them . . .

I was not interested in sheet music. I began to hang about the house, and when she was not around I would play the piano, though always playing up in "the tinkles."

I had created a beautiful piece of music. It was a classical waltz with melody and accompaniment. My mother walked into the room, catching me by surprise.

"I know what this is," she said snarlingly.

"I made it up," I replied.

"No, you didn't," she retorted. "That's Beethoven."

It was meant to be an insult, but she never knew how much she had complimented me. I guess I couldn't blame her for her jealousy. It seemed I had the Midas touch for all the things she so admired and at which her sister so excelled: artistic and creative ability.

My mother satisfied her own insecurity by emphasizing that people who played by ear could not learn to read music. She began to take music lessons and, in fierce competition with her daughter, who was in no way trying to compete, she did extremely well.

As if to prove her point, she took me for an introductory music lesson. The woman teacher told me to forget entirely anything I "thought" I knew about music. She was there, it seemed, to undo such bad learning habits and teach me the discipline of music "properly."

Predictably I would not follow the teacher's instructions and would not cooperate. Satisfied, my mother gloated viciously over my obvious "failure." Five years later I bought my own piano and began to compose.

The piano had been my only renewed interest at home, but the jealousy my playing had inspired again made life at home intolerable. My mother, however, began to phone me at my friend's house, commanding I come home. I'd travel several suburbs back home, she'd send me out to the shop at the end of the street, then tell me I was free to return to my friend's house.

IIII

ANY TIME I spent at home I spent in my room listening to records. Like so many other teenagers, I would turn the record up as loud as possible, sing at the top of my voice and play the same record over and over again.

I had drawn spirals on all of my records and would sit watching these wind themselves in. At other times I would place objects on the records, experimenting with the speed control until the objects would go flying across the record and sometimes across the room.

Like at school, I would imitate my records, singing them at various speeds. When I was home, I was driving everybody mad.

My little brother would try to enter my room. I'd almost scream the house down. My mother would come up and she'd scream the house down. One day my father came up to try to talk to me.

It was the first time in my life that he had come into my room to talk to me. He tried to make conversation. He asked me about the records I was listening to. I played some of the songs that had special meaning for me. I never explained why; this was one of the only real efforts I'd made at trying to share how I felt with anyone in my family.

My father had all the right responses; he simply sat within my presence, letting me show him how I felt in the only way I could—via objects. He came back several times, and I eventually had the courage to show him some of the secret pictures I'd drawn and the poems I'd written.

He wanted, I suppose, so much to bridge the gap between the members of the family that he made one fatal mistake. He not only praised the quality of my work, but did so in front of somebody who was not included in my efforts to share: my mother.

Cuttingly my mother insisted that I show her what I'd written. I handed over my poems, and she mockingly read some of what I had written out loud, criticizing the grammar, the images I had used, and "its madness." "It's typical," she said, as though that summed up everything. Fortunately, in the evasiveness of my so-called "mad" writing, its meaning eluded her; and so, to my mind, it remained "uncontaminated" by "informed" criticism. My father looked at me apologetically. I guess he was something of an eternal optimist.

My father had never laid a hand on me. Despite this, my mother sought to convince me that my father was "looking at me." I was always so easily fooled, often believing the most unbelievable things, only to be made a fool of later. I began to ignore my father as my mother so actively encouraged. Sadly it was the last effort at reaching me that my father was to make for three years.

||||

AT SCHOOL THE other children had begun to pick on me. I'd become fairly insensitive to being called mad but I was now being called stupid, and though I was quite aware of my own naïveté, this still hurt. As always, I reacted violently, though this time my opponents were boys.

My mother, in sympathy for the way I was being attacked, gave me one last chance at another school. This time it was to be on her terms. I was now fourteen years old, and I was going to go to a girls' school.

||||

SEXUALITY HAD ALWAYS disturbed me, probably because of how claustrophobic I felt when other people came near me. My mother, who was extremely paranoid about me becoming a teenage mother, took every available opportunity to put me down and physically abuse me for any signs of my femininity.

In some ways her fears were justified. I was extremely naïve and believed anything I was told. I often went off with strangers, enticed down lanes and toward strange cars by lures of saving poor starving kittens or getting sweets. Fortunately it had always been another, very characteristic part of my nature that saved me from any real harm: my complete dislike of physical proximity and being touched. I may never have screamed, but if anyone tried to touch me I ran like hell. However, at this particular time the comments of other girls were worrying me.

I had occasionally actually wanted to be spoken to by boys I met. These boys, however, were always the quiet ones who never approached me, and so I never spoke to them. At the same time, other boys were, I suppose, attracted to my naïveté. I was easily led and easily conned and was easy pickings for egocentric bullying types who got a kick out of how evasive I became. I was already well skilled in the art of kicking such beasts where it hurt, but my increasing need to appear to be coping and "normal" meant that I put my friend's mother's lessons about tolerating affection to very bad use.

As I was completely unable to say, let alone acknowledge, what I did or didn't want, boys found that they could mentally corner me. I had nevertheless grown up in a house full of strangers and parties, and was skilled in evasiveness if not in emotional self-defense.

A rough school can put forward many challenges to the "normality" of a teenager's sexual development, and the girls' school I had been sent to was no exception. The girls at this school would leer at passing strangers, compare notes on their experiences, and talk about their latest heartthrob.

I was never communicative, but owing to my background, I always became anxious about challenges to my "normality." The old fear was still there, always driving me to try to keep at least one foot in the "real world" lest I be sent to my mind's conception of irretrievable hell on earth: a children's home.

||||

ONE COULD, I suppose, blame my mother for putting the fear of imprisonment into my head. Then again, it was my mind, not hers, that conjured up the monstrous connotations of the words. To me, a children's home was a prison, and I was absolutely terrified of outside control.

I did not fear that my arms and legs would be ripped off in a children's home. They would have been welcome to take them with my blessing. I was terrified that they would make me *do* things there; that they would not leave me be; that they would deny me my freedom to escape into my own lonely, though secure, prison.

When I locked myself in, I locked other people out. In my own family I felt I still had reasonable control over this. At the same time, it was the very threat of having my circumstances changed (no matter how bad they may have seemed) that made me try so hard to convince people that I was capable of their precious "normality." It was this that, so strongly against my own will, caused me to fight so hard for so little reward for the joyless achievement of remaining aware and responsive.

It was this fear of having "my own world" taken away from me that resulted in behavior that forced me to deny "my own world" in place of a more presentable, well-mannered, sociable, though emotionless, shell. "They" never got to lay a hand on the real me, but more and more, to their elation, I began to stop visiting myself.

I began to stop looking at the spots and losing myself in the colors. I began to lose a grip on my love of the things around me and, in doing so, was left with "their" shallow securities and complete lack of guarantees. My hatred became my only realness, and when I was not angry, I said sorry for breathing, for taking up space, and even began to say sorry for saying sorry. This total denial of a right to live was a consequence of learning to act normal. Everything outside of me told me that my survival was to rest on my refining the act of acting normal. On the inside I knew that by definition this meant that whatever and whoever I was naturally was unworthy of acceptance, belonging, or even life.

IIII

MY HISTORY AT this last school was the same as at the others. I was a failure. I still failed to participate, or did so inappropriately. I still walked out of classes, threw things, and got violent. I still failed to hand in any work at all, with one exception.

I had liked one of my teachers, which was quite unusual for me as I normally either disliked them or was indifferent to them. Liking anyone, however, posed major difficulties for me, as it made me far more nervous and left me more unprepared than when dealing with someone I disliked. I don't know why I liked this teacher, perhaps it was because she seemed to have little "self" about her.

She was always talking about what had happened throughout history to various disadvantaged groups. Nothing she ever said had any feeling of stubbornness, bias, or opinion. She simply discussed facts.

I found it impossible to talk to her in a normal voice. I began to put on a strong American accent, making up a history and identity for myself to go with it. As always, I actually convinced myself that I was this new character and consistently kept this up for six months.

While the other teachers found me a devil, this teacher found me to be bright, amusing, and a pleasure to teach. At the end of the term, I handed her the most important piece of schoolwork any of my high school teachers had received.

The students had all been given a set date and topic on which to write. I had been intrigued by the way black people had been treated in America in the sixties.

I told my teacher that what I wanted to do was a secret, and she agreed to extend my due date as I enthusiastically informed her of the growing length of my project. I had gone through every book I could find on the topic, cutting out pictures and drawing illustrations over my written pages, as I had always done, to capture the feel of what I wanted to write about. The other students had given her projects spanning an average of about three pages in length. I proudly gave her my special project of twenty-six pages, illustrations, and drawings. She gave me an A, and I shyly, though immediately, dropped the American accent.

In all my high school years, this was my greatest achievement. I had, of course, done this project not so much out of my own interests as in an effort to win this teacher's approval. Unfortunately, this tendency is one I have been largely unable to overcome.

IIII

MY MOTHER DECIDED that it was time for me to get a job. I was fifteen years old.

I had been the housecleaner and done cleaning jobs for my father. I was also very keen on sewing. It was a toss-up between being a cleaner or a machinist. I began my first full-time job as a machinist and lasted exactly three days.

Though I am now opposed to the killing of animals for fur coats, I still loved the feel of fur at that time and made no connection between a live animal and a fur coat. I had always had difficulty with the concept of something being turned into something else. I understood cows, but when they became a herd they stopped being cows for me. I understood that "herd" was a word used for a group but did not understand the word "cattle." Fur was like that, too. Once it was being sewn, it was material and had never been and could never be animals.

What I did know is that I loved the feel of fur on my face. I was a runny-nosed, freckle-faced, fifteen-year-old kid rubbing her face into fur coats with no conception of or respect for their value or for the notion that they were supposed to stand for "class."

The boss was Italian and, like so many Italians, was a hard

worker and expected the same of his employees. I was to begin on the easiest of machines: the buttonholer.

The buttonhole machine cuts a hole in the garment and then stitches around the hole it has made. It was magic. I was fascinated by the feel of fur under my hands. I was in paradise.

I worked hard and I worked fast. Soon the box of fur coats began to fill up, and the boss passed by, impressed with the speed of my work. He decided to check the quality.

A horrified look grew upon his face, and he began to shout as he turned each garment around and around.

"What have you done?" he screamed over and over. "Buttonholes in the sleeves, buttonholes in the collar, buttonholes in the back panel . . . Get the hell out of here."

"Can I have my money?" I asked shyly.

"No!" he screamed. "Do you know what you've done? You've caused me thousands of dollars in damage. Get the hell out of here before I kick you out."

I hadn't realized that the buttonholes were meant to go anywhere in particular.

IIII

I WAS ABLE to apply myself much better to a full-time job than I ever was to schoolwork. At school I had never had one consistent identity, and my behavior was all over the place. In my new job I was given an image, and the whole point seemed to be to be true to this role at all times.

My form of concentration was never to be alert, as this would cause me to drift off. Instead I would lose myself in the monotonous tasks I was given to do. I moved so freely and systematically through my work that most people hardly noticed my very distant state of mind.

I had been very lucky, I was told, at having landed a job as a shop assistant in a department store. I loved my job but hated dealing with people.

It seemed that I was again in paradise, surrounded by racks and shelves of colored garments, shiny shoes, rows of numerically ordered packages. Everything was arranged in aisles. It seemed almost unbelievable that I would be expected to do the thing I loved most: put things in order. There were numbers to be counted and ordered, there were colors and sizes and types of article to be grouped; every department was kept separate from every other department and called by a different name; it was a world of guarantees, and this department store even offered those, too.

I was the best little worker they had, I was told. Heads of various departments would ask to "borrow" me to tidy up the mess in their departments, which I would do in record time, in every detail. I was the sort of kid who vacuumed the floor by hand without the help of a vacuum cleaner. If there was anything slightly out of place, I had to straighten it; and doing this, restoring order, made me feel secure. Despite this, I was being continually reminded of my "attitude problem."

Customers would approach me for help, and I would completely ignore them. As this was my most important role as a shop assistant, my bosses could never overlook this. When I did help them, I often did it with such bitter resentment that customers would complain to management about the rude girl in such and such department.

Sometimes the customers would tap me on the shoulder. I'd tell them to wait a minute, as I continued compulsively to sort out racks and shelves. If they persisted, I would abruptly remind them that I had told them to wait. People sometimes couldn't believe my arrogance.

However, I was not being intentionally arrogant. These people had, uninvited, tried to take away my control over being touched, though to them it was a mere tap on the shoulder. These were the people who, out of their own selfishness, would rob me of my sense of peace and security, which, unlike them, I could not find in their version of "everyday life."

As people began to explain how other people experienced my behavior, I came to learn that all behavior had two definitions: theirs and mine. These "helpful" people were trying to help me to "overcome my ignorance" yet they never tried to understand the way I saw the world. It seemed so simple to them. There were rules. The rules were right. I obviously needed their help to learn them.

IIII

THERE WAS ALSO another problem: the way I spoke.

I would often fluctuate between accents and pitches and would vary the manner in which I described things. Sometimes my accent seemed quite polished and refined. Sometimes I spoke as though I was born and bred in the gutter. Sometimes my pitch was normal, at other times it was deep, like I was doing an Elvis impersonation. When I was excited, however, it sounded like Mickey Mouse after being run over by a steamroller—high pitched and flat.

Someone didn't know the price of a soft toy. I was told to get on the microphone and ask for its price and code. I was nervous and excited. I was going to say something on the microphone that would be heard over the entire store.

I looked at what I was to describe. I saw a yellow stuffed duck. Whether polished and refined or subtle as a sledgehammer, I had always been notorious for bluntly telling it like I saw it. I got on the microphone and in a very loud, flat, high-pitched drawl demanded: "Give me a price and code on a yellow stuffed duck."

Laughter poured forth from the walls. The entire shop seemed to be laughing. I walked back to where I had been working, wondering what had happened since I'd been gone that had made everyone laugh.

My boss glared at me, mortified.

"What did you say?" she announced in disbelief.

"When?" I asked.

"On the microphone, you stupid girl," she added.

I was called up to the office.

"Donna, we've got a new job for you. We're sure you'll like it," said the assistant manager, sitting behind his desk, hands clasped, looking like a ridiculous praying mantis.

"But I don't want another job," I said innocently.

"We've decided that you should go and work in the store-room. You'll like it in there," he added, sounding like he was convincing himself, for I certainly didn't feel convinced.

||||

THE STOREROOM WAS dark, a long corridor with other long dark corridors running off it. Like the rest of the store, every-thing was divided up into separate sections. There was neat-ness and order, but a lot of the prettiness was missing. Nevertheless I was content with the isolation. With this now being the domain of my boss and myself alone, I began to treat it as such.

People often came into the storeroom to see if something was in stock. I began to close the door on people, trying to keep them out. Then I'd walk away back to what I was doing.

I was extremely possessive of my tidying and would go off like a firecracker if anyone left anything out of order.

I had also decided that I would take orders from one per-son and one person only. One day my boss's boss came in, the store manager. He began to talk to me. I had become upset about something and was huddled in a ball down one of the long corridors.

My own boss had been unable to approach me, as I had picked up the merchandise and hurled articles at her like missiles. She had arrived with the manager as a backup. I went berserk. Like some insane little pixie, I stamped my feet, pulled out my hair, screamed, and threw things at both of them before giving up and banging my head rhythmically on the shelf next to me. There was nowhere to go from the storeroom but out of the exit. Fortunately my boss talked the manager around, and I was not out of a job. She managed to explain that I couldn't take orders from more than one person.

Like Robyn's mother, my boss had seen me as a wayward child in need of guidance. She didn't realize that I was already functioning in line with a very stringent set of rules that were not compatible with life as a secure, well-adjusted social being.

IIII

OUTSIDE WORK, I had, like so many times before, cut myself off from the people I knew, some of whom had grown quite fond of me.

I had begun to skate, which was something that gave me a great sense of freedom and beauty. I felt untouchable as I sped around the skating rink, people becoming a momentary blur of color as I whizzed past them. Like everything else, I had taught myself well and, dancing alone, oblivious to everyone else around me, I began to attract attention.

A young man approached me and began to skate around with me. As always, boys would comment on how well I skated or challenge me to defend myself by saying that I thought I was good. Some would skate around me, trying to be impressive. I was not easily impressed, and I was not particularly impressed by this young man. After the usual blah blah blah, he offered to walk me home. I accepted.

I walked ahead of Garry most of the way, and he didn't seem to acknowledge my evasiveness. I stood at the front gate, not particularly wanting to go inside. He kept saying words. I replied: Yes, sir. No, sir. Three bags full, sir. He kissed me—or perhaps I should say he kissed my face, as I wasn't in it at the time.

I met Garry almost every night when I went to the rink. He said he loved me. Echoing, I said I loved him, too. He wanted me to come and live with him one day. Me, too, I said. He kissed my face again.

Well, I'd said the words; it must have been love. He wanted me to live with him. Great! I didn't want to live at home anymore. I would go and live at his place.

I called a taxi and filled it up with my bags and tins full of treasures, my stereo and records and the few clothes that I had bought for myself since I had been working. I arrived at Garry's flat and, to his flatmate's complete surprise, moved in.

Garry arrived home to the sheepish grin of his flatmate's girlfriend, who informed him that I'd moved in.

"What!" he exclaimed in disbelief.

"You said you wanted me to live with you," I explained.

"One day, I said," he stressed.

Nevertheless, I was there, and that was that.

My mother freaked out entirely. She had a strange feeling about my absence and checked my room to find I'd taken everything personal, leaving the place with the eeriness of a mortuary. The bare floor, wall-to-wall mirrors, the barred windows, and a hoard of untouched, unwanted dolls spoke of who I was. My mother stood there among the rejected dolls and, so she told me, cried for the first time.

I had no intention of returning. It was not that I thought I'd found the love of my life. I was not particularly excited about the adventure of leaving home. I had simply been invited (or so it had appeared to me) to take the next step along the road to independence, which I thought was synonymous with being left alone. I had a lot to learn.

I did not particularly want to share this man's bed or have sex with him. I was disturbed and anxious about the changes that had taken place during the day and didn't want to be on my own, though I'd have been happier if my company had been deaf, dumb, blind, and indifferent to me. He wasn't.

At first Garry was furious with me. He told me that he didn't particularly want to live with me, but that it was too late now and he'd have to learn to live with it. For my part, I found it useful to play my old role of Carol, always willing to please, anything to avoid being sent away. Garry was an immature and insecure adult. He thought this pliant role suited me, and he learned to make use of it as one would a household utensil.

I was not particularly thrilled about sex. I had decided my body didn't belong to me at all. I felt it was something quite separate from me, numb; my eyes staring into nothingness and my mind a thousand miles away. I felt somehow killed and yet somehow free by being so cut off and unreachable. And in some perverse way I'm sure Garry liked having a victim instead of a partner. I understood that sex was a condition of my staying with him. He created many new conditions, too. He was to receive all of the money that I brought home from work, and I was never to ask for anything or complain. I tried to argue for the money for my fares to work and soon learned that life was no better living in a relationship than it was living at home. Just as my mother had, Garry began to bash me night after night.

There were four of us altogether, and we moved into a house with one other: a man named Ron, recently separated from his wife.

The violence still went on night after night. I'd hide in a corner, huddling, holding my head. It was cat-and-mouse, and there was nowhere to hide. Sometimes the others would tell Garry to close the door while he hit me because he was making too much noise.

One night I sat up in the living room, again too afraid to go to sleep; now frightened by both the bashing and the darkness. The darkness in my soul, however, was the greatest, and I sat there staring vacantly into space, tearing my arm up with a nail I had found.

Ron came in. He sat next to me and, in my dazed state, I thought he was trying to understand. He said I could come out with him driving in his van. I went.

Ron pulled over to the side of the road and told me that if I wanted to go home I would have to have sex with him. I opened the van door, got out, and began walking up the road, out in the middle of nowhere, with no idea of where I was going.

"Get back in the van," he said through the open window as he drove slowly along beside me.

I continued to walk.

"You don't know where you are," he said.

"Don't care," I said bluntly.

"Come on, get in the van. You won't have to do anything," he said.

I continued to walk.

"You're mad, you know that," he said. "You're stark raving mad."

Eventually I got back into the van, and he drove me home without incident.

The next day I walked around the block, hypnotized by the monotony of going around and around and around again. I heard only the rhythm of my own footsteps and saw only the blur of the houses that, like the people at the skating rink, whizzed past me. As I did this, I tore apart the inside of my arm—the part of my body my friend Robyn had taught me to feel.

There was a couple staying in the house, Garry's cousin and his pregnant fifteen-year-old girlfriend. The inside of my arm was a mass of blood and pus and torn flesh. The eight-months-pregnant girlfriend couldn't stand the atmosphere anymore. Her boyfriend decided that the violence had gone too far. It was time to get out of there. They decided to move into Garry's sister's flat. Out of sympathy, the girlfriend insisted I come with them.

Garry's sister had a flat a few suburbs away. She lived there with her three-year-old daughter in a neighborhood teeming with cats. The couple were to sleep in the daughter's bedroom. The daughter was to sleep with her mother. I was to sleep on the living room floor after any visitors had gone.

I had no mattress, pillows, or blankets. I was allowed to use the cushions off the couch after everyone had gone to sleep. I put my treasures in the linen cupboard next to where I lay, covered myself with a towel, and went to sleep.

||||

GARRY'S SISTER WAS very like him. I gave her most of my wages and almost all of the rest to the couple, in exchange for their offer to take me with them when they moved up-country in a few weeks' time after their baby was born. On top of this, I looked after Garry's sister's daughter after I got home from work and on weekends.

There was never any food in the house, although half of the money I'd given this woman was intended for food. I went to work in my job in the storeroom and watched people eat. When people asked me why I didn't eat, I told them I wasn't hungry. People offered me some of their food. I scoffed it down like a wild dog. Some of the women at work got into the habit of buying themselves too much for lunch and giving me what they'd bought. Their kindness brought tears to my eyes, and I ate gratefully, with the tears silently rolling down my cheeks.

At home in the flat my only salvation was that little girl, and she became the entire world for me. I would take her with me everywhere, and almost everything she did I did, too.

It was as though I had a playmate my own age. At times I was in a dream state possibly not even as complex as the world seen by a three-year-old. At other times, as I was beginning to come out of myself, being three with this little girl felt about all that I could handle without my defenses distorting my self-expression and leaving me a thousand miles away from who I really was.

I had spent my last birthday away from home. My family had given me a set of colored pencils. I sat looking at them intently, alone in the flat I was sharing, and felt deeply hurt that I no longer could allow myself to draw in color, for the self-expression of using color demonstrated choice and inspired too much fear. I cried as I clung to a tiny doll on a string that my little brother had given me.

I had begun to get quite sick, and under my nervous painted smile it was quite clear that I was extremely depressed.

Up until now I had refused to have much to do with my family. My father had been deeply hurt by my leaving and had begun to snub me when I phoned, nervously waiting to be asked if I wanted to come back home. My two brothers had rejected me as someone who had, it seemed, proved to them that they were as worthless as discarded rubbish. My mother, who had told anyone who asked that I'd left because I was a slut, was, for a change, more understanding. Charitably she invited me to come back. I agreed. I had been gone three months. It was Christmastime.

||||

I WAS NOW sixteen years old. My family, which had often felt so very foreign to me, now felt even more so. I hung about on the fringes like an outsider. My presence at Christmas had been unexpected, but I still received presents from people. The presents from my parents' friends and relatives hurt most. Although they had often given me Christmas presents, I felt they were making a special effort toward me, and I couldn't face them or even bring myself to say thank you. I simply felt too fragile.

||||

MY OLDER BROTHER had begun teasing me, and I began teasing him back. Things got out of hand, and I was on the receiving end. My mother decided that it was time for me to move out.

I had been home for only three months. My mother knew I'd lost all of my money and came into the shop where I was working. She threw a bank book at me. In it she had deposited the cost of the security bond on a flat. I got home and she threw the newspaper in front of me, telling me to find myself a flat. I found one two suburbs away and, because I was still only sixteen, she came with me to the real estate agent and gave them her assurance that I would be able to pay my rent.

I had left my job as a storeroom assistant and taken a job in a factory near my flat. I had come full circle and was now working the dreaded buttonhole machine again. I lived on my own and felt proud of the way I was taking control over my own life, but I was terribly lonely.

Every night I would walk barefoot down to the local shop and telephone my old friend Robyn, with whom I had still intermittently stayed in touch. I would phone up with nothing to say and ask her "So how are you?" about ten times before saying goodnight and hanging up. Her mother had always enjoyed showing me off as her charity project, and the novelty of that had begun to wear off for me.

I had been walking back home after one of these phone calls when a group of boys my own age who hung about outside the shop began to harass me. I guess I looked like an easy target for harassment, as I was always out making phone calls at the same time each night, barefoot, in the same long, oversized saggy jumper, come rain or shine. I'd never talk to them or look at them. I'd just walk straight back home. For kicks, they decided to follow me.

The three of them walked directly behind me. I was frightened. I opened the door of my flat, and one of them put his hand on the door, holding it open.

"Aren't you going to invite us in?" he asked.

"Get out," I said frightened.

"That's not very nice," he said. "I think we'll come in and take a look around."

With that the three of them entered my flat as though they owned it.

"What have you got here?" one said, opening up my kitchen cupboards one by one.

"Please get out of here," I pleaded, as they went through the contents of my cupboards, laughing at my poverty and mocking my vulnerability.

I became so scared that I went and stood outside my own front door. The three gave up, cheekily strutting out the front door one by one, laughing. The last one announced that he needed to "take a piss," which he promptly did, in full view, on my front door.

I stood there horrified as the three of them proudly strutted off. That night I put on my best dress, took a handful of sleeping pills, played my favorite record, and danced around the flat. Dazed, I caught a glimpse of my reflection in the mirror and began, like all those years ago, to talk to Carol. I began to cry, and all I knew was that I didn't want to be there anymore. Hypnotically I began to cut my wrists as I stood in front of the mirror.

The look on my own face was too much. It wasn't Carol looking back anymore. I panicked.

Willie stood in front of the mirror thinking that, if I died, people would see me dressed like that, like a pretty little girl. I took off my dress and put on my old jumper. As Willie, I ripped a sheet and wound the scraps around my wrists and fell asleep.

When I awoke it was clear that I needed help. Carol had no intention of telling anyone what had happened, but she could no longer face the mess in the flat. I put on my jeans and walked, at six o'clock in the morning, up to my friend Robyn's place.

Robyn's mum answered the door.

"Hello, pet," she said. "What's the matter?"

"Nothing," said Carol, laughing lightheartedly. "Just thought I'd come down for a visit."

Carol sat at the kitchen table while she made me the customary cup of tea. I had begun to bleed through my jumper, and Robyn's mum looked at me in shock, saying: "What have you done?" Knowing that I might run if she panicked, she calmly asked if she might take a look at my arms. Carol complied, explaining that she'd had a little accident. Robyn's mother explained that these "scratches" might get infected and asked me to let them take me to the hospital. Carol agreed to let Robyn take me there. Everybody was calm, cool, and collected. The nurse came and spoke to me. The doctors took blood tests. I was given food to eat and lots to drink, and when I told them I was ready to go they told me I was not. I was made to see a psychiatrist.

Mary, my psychiatrist, didn't frighten me. She seemed to be a firm but gentle person who didn't react to whatever images I tried to throw at her. She asked me why I'd done what I'd done. I told her it was because "there was no love left in the world."

She sat across from Willie and told me that she didn't think that I was as tough as I thought I was and that she thought there was a scared little girl inside me who was trying to get out. I wondered if she knew how right she was. Willie spent a year thinking about what she had said.

IIII

I RETURNED TO the flat and the factory and the ritual telephone calls from outside the local shop. A tall, lanky man sat on a crate outside the shop. This was the local haunt, and this was his usual spot. A friend and he were paying a lot of attention to me as I made my usual phone calls.

"Hi, how are you, so how are you, yeah . . . yeah . . . yeah . . ." I said on the phone.

"Hi," called the young man as I hung up and walked past, ignoring him. "Aren't you going to be friendly and talk to me?" he persisted.

His friend interrupted, suggesting that I ask the young man, Chris, back to my place for coffee.

"I haven't got coffee," I replied.

"That's okay," said his friend. "He'll take tea."

It seemed to be settled as far as these two were concerned. Chris was to come to my place for a cup of tea.

I walked into my own flat ahead of him, almost oblivious to his presence. He took a seat on my fifteen-dollar couch from the Salvation Army and made himself quite at home.

"I haven't got any tea," I explained.

"That's okay," said Chris. "I'll just stay for the conversation." He hung around making one.

Chris was Italian and lived around the corner from my flat. He had noticed the bandages on my wrists, and I told him that I had sprained them doing a handstand. He didn't believe me. I told him about the incident with the three guys, which had led up to my "accident." As it turned out, the one who had urinated on my front door was his younger brother.

I move from place to place, a life of nameless faces,
Looking for some place that I'd call home,

I'd always be moving on;
Always trying to find some place I could call mine,
But that never came my way and the feeling was here to stay,
Not knowing who I used to be.
I look in the mirror, in the face looking back I see . . .
"Don't know. Who is me?"

I gave Chris a key to my flat, and he made good use of it, throwing parties and referring to it as his flat. I sat about, a stranger in my own flat, watching Chris bring the world in mercilessly as he played the playboy role to a T.

My flat got flooded from a blockage in the flats' sewerage. I stood there screaming. The landlord stood there saying, "Not a problem. We'll clean it up with a mop." The estate agent agreed that he wouldn't allow a dog to sleep in those conditions. I was given another, though more expensive, flat.

Chris's friend, Peter, moved into the spare room. He taught me to cook and to iron clothes and, being quite a giant, he would throw me up into the air and catch me. I'd fall to the ground laughing, and he'd tickle me as I wildly came to life.

Life moved fast, and I moved even faster. It wasn't long before I had left this flat far behind, and Peter with it. I was saying words, taking actions, but I wasn't there.

I moved every two months, and when I wasn't moving house I changed jobs. Chris would see the cardboard boxes laid out on the bed and realize that I was moving again.

I spent my spare time inspecting new flats, though never moving outside the one suburb. I lost a fortune in security deposits, but I felt compelled to move as two months in one place had begun to feel like two very long years.

Living as Carol, completely cut off from my real self and the emotions it embodied, I became terrified of being left alone. I feared becoming possessed by the real me, which seemed to lurk in the shadows like a ghost, waiting for Carol to be left alone, waiting for life to slow down and catch up with her.

I played the role of Carol so convincingly that I hardly acknowledged that this fear was my fear of losing a grip on this character. I had played Carol so persistently that she had become a self. My little brother came around to see me. But Carol had no brother Tom.

Tell me, do you remember me? Do I look like I belong?
See, I've been looking around,
To find a face in the crowd that I might know.
Do you have the time for one more friend?
Do I have a face you'd like to know?
Well, we might just start there,
It's as good a place as anywhere.

Tom had come to the door of the flat. Carol opened the door and stood their staring at the figure of a ten-year-old boy on the doorstep. Having not seen me for almost a year, Tom probably remembered the real me, Donna, who had shared her world with him when he was three. The girl who answered the door was the one who had walked away from him—and from everything else in her life—because there was too much closeness to handle.

"Hi, sis," Tom announced as he stood on the doorstep, dwarfed by his older sister.

"Hi. What do you want?" said the seventeen-year-old facing him.

"Mum brought me down. She's out in front. Do you want to see her?" he said.

"Nuh," said the girl flippantly. "Want to come in?"

"I can't," said Tom. "Mum's asked me to come and ask you to see her," he added.

"Oh, well, tell her I can't," said the girl casually. "I guess you'd better go."

Tom went. It was his last visit for two years.

Chris had moved in. He liked the latest flat. Carol brought out the cardboard boxes, but Chris refused to move with her. Carol was now on a trapeze that had begun to swing without mercy. Donna's older brother entered the scene before Carol's last curtain call.

The older brother had never liked Donna. She'd always been hard to understand and never seemed to say anything he could make sense of. He was, however, going through his own teenage years; an adult way before his time, alone and lonely. For better or for worse, he decided there was now some advantage in reaching out to his sister. He was greeted by Carol.

He sat on the couch, talking to the charming and captivating character who sat there masquerading as his sister. I had switched to "automatic pilot," and watched myself from outside my own body as I responded openly and effortlessly to the brother I had never had any desire to get to know.

It seemed to him that he had found a friend who was almost made to order. Fortunately, his sister had changed. This girl had no longing look for understanding, and spoke casually and amusingly without any of the distrust or cautiousness he had known in his sister. He liked her, and decided to come around more often.

It was as though I had been watching a play, although I was simultaneously in the audience and on the stage. But as my older brother continued to visit, Carol began to falter, finding it increasingly difficult to communicate. Donna had reverted to "talking in poetry" evasively.

Playfully my brother began once again to call me "a blonk" and told me to stop "wonking." I froze as though he were a nightmare come to life. He was again calling me mad, stupid, and incomprehensible. I looked at him, wondering at how he had come to feel so comfortable in my flat. He eventually began to realize that this was no mere mood I was in. I had gone back to being the same way I used to be, and he had better things to do with his time than waste any more of it on his "crazy" sister who seemed to resent or ignore his company. My older brother didn't drop in again until two years later, when we were once again enemies as always.

IIII

Donna was the ghost, and the ghost was back. People, however, had come to expect Carol, and Carol put up a fight.

I had become agoraphobic. I tried to walk to the local shops. I would shake, feeling my knees give out from under me. I was again a frightened caged animal, running from and flinching at any efforts to come near me, though clutching at Chris as the only adult who could protect me from the invasion of the outside world.

I became unable to work, running out on jobs without explanation. I began to tremble and feel like I was going to faint. In panic I would look around my once familiar surroundings, unable to make sense of them or why I had forced myself to be there. Carol would sail through each job interview, but Donna would run out on the job after every few weeks.

I developed two nervous tics, and would break out in a purple rash that covered my chest, neck, and half of my face every time I was approached on or spoke about any emotionally laden topic.

Chris was unable to cope and began to go out every night. One day he announced that he was going away for the weekend.

I was in a state of panic. Chris's going away was like the feeling of desertion I had had when my grandfather had died when I was five. At the same time I had to paint a smile upon my tear-soaked face and wave bye-bye with my best impression of the Carol he had grown fond of. I was not convincing. Carol had progressed to being a teenager, but Donna was still only two years old at a stretch.

I sat alone in the flat, deserted and terrified. I needed a mother desperately, but could not remember ever having one; and, truth be known, this, too, would have to be a construction within my own world, if it were not to send me running. I felt homesick for the home I'd never had because I'd never been able to reach out freely.

Carol had brought Chris into my life. Giggling, sociable, and made to order, Carol had become all he expected and demanded, yet he had walked out on Donna as though she were a complete stranger. I remembered the words of another complete stranger that had been echoing in my mind since meeting her the year before. I went to the emergency room of the hospital and asked to see Mary, the psychiatrist who had been able to see the frightened little girl inside me trying to get out.

IIII

I WAS CALLED into the cubicle of the emergency room and seen by an insensitive orderly who tried to insist that I could not see Mary and that I was just a little bit upset and would soon be fine.

Words were to be my only chance, and Willie's complete lack of tact came viciously to the rescue. His eyes raced around the cubicle, scanning it for objects that could be thrown. He verbally assaulted the unsuspecting orderly with attacks of "What do I have to do? Tear this room to bits, cut myself up and bleed everywhere?" The orderly arranged for Mary to see me.

Mary and Willie sat in the office across the table from one another. I was fighting to break the surface of the character who sat there desperately trying to defend me and, at the same time, defeating the purpose of getting help.

Willie explained the nature of the problem at hand in a relatively calm and controlled way. It was explained to Mary that the problem was an inability to trust Chris while he was away and that this was causing pressure on the relationship. Mary, testing the water, questioned my own ability to be trusted and then asked me what my family had been like.

The rash began to creep, and I could sense emotion creeping to the surface with it. "What does that have to do with anything?" Willie asked rather defensively in a last-ditch effort to clutch at straws that might temporarily block my encroaching fragility. He was wasting time in order to think up a new strategy. Mary explained that it had a lot to do with things and asked me once again about my family. Willie began to describe my family situation with the objectivity with which one would narrate the moves of a sporting event.

Mary left the room. I panicked. By the time she came back I was a crying, babbling mess. She suggested we meet again the next day.

It was Sunday. I had only one more day to get through before the whole world would once again come through my front door in the form of Chris.

I bought some strawberries on the way to the hospital, from the shop at the end of the street, and entered the hospital waiting room, where I waited to be called. Donna was called into the office; Carol, carrying the bag of strawberries, entered.

Carol was always sent out to test the water before Donna decided it was safe to jump in. Mary and I ate the strawberries. Tokenistic as the gesture to offer them may have been, Mary had accepted them and got past the first hurdle. My fears began to emerge.

"I'm not mad, you know, am I?" said Carol, hoping that Mary would not confirm the fear that I actually was. Mary was always reassuring, telling me that I need not worry so much about it.

"They're not going to lock me up, are they?" asked Carol, echoing the old fear of being sent to a children's home.

"No, you're not going to get locked up," echoed Mary.

My fears broke the surface, and I began to sob like a child.

It was arranged that I would see Mary twice a week for the first couple of weeks. These weeks were to stretch on into months and then into years. Mary was to become the most important mental influence on my life since I met that stranger named Carol in the park fourteen years before.

An adult trapped in a child's insecurity,
Seeming complete, and yet not,
To open its eyes to a world never seen,
And hear the sound of people,
As though for the first time, without fear,

To express in its own words gratification,
And to feel in its heart some of the security it's longed for
Is a gift.
What better gift than to give someone their self?

Mary had asked me what I expected to get out of the sessions. I had told her: "I just wanna be normal." I had never questioned the concept of normal but I felt that I didn't fit the category by a long shot.

We almost always sat in the same office; the same view, overlooking the city street and the park across the road. When it was nighttime, I would look out at the city lights, and sometimes, in my mind, I would feel as I might have done in one of my flying dreams, this time moving through the blackness to the colors.

This office symbolized my dilemma. I was stuck in a small room of brightness, and the rest of the world was a beckoning but unreachable light that lay miles beyond a terrifying journey through the dark. Mary was to help guide me there. At home I would draw pictures of this over and over again in my diary: a white square within a larger black square, surrounded everywhere by the blinding whiteness of the paper.

Recently I saw this picture again. It had been drawn by a young autistic girl and was featured in a book by a psychoanalyst who worked with such children. The adult analysis of the picture was that it expressed this girl's longing for the breast. When, after becoming close to her counselor, she drew two white squares in the darkness, this was interpreted as two breasts. When she then reversed the picture, with a black square now in the middle of the white paper, this was taken to be her version of the "bad breast" as opposed to the "good breast."

I laughed myself stupid when I read this. I had drawn the same picture over and over, writing beside it, "Get me the hell out of here." This was the symbolic representation of my trap, which was due to the infantile nature of my unreached emotions. The blackness I had to get through was the jump between "my world" and "the world," though I had never been able to make it in one piece. I had learned to fear the complete loss of all attachment to my emotional self, which happened when I made the jump, and this was the only way that communication was possible. Giving up the secret of this was simply too deadly. Too many well-meaning people would have tried mercilessly to drag me through the darkness unprepared, killing my emotional self in the process. I may never have died physically, but psychically I had died many times in the effort. I had multiple fractures of the soul as a result.

||||

THE ENTIRE PSYCHIATRIC outpatient department was bland and colorless. In a way, that made me safe. It was like a huge room of nothingness with other little rooms of nothingness dotted along the corridors. Mary's office had a picture on the wall, two chairs, and a desk. The picture was bland and washed out, the sort that was meant to make patients feel calm. I remember looking at this picture and finding nothing in it that I could mentally grasp. Even the colors, which were a mass of bland, dull pastels, blended into one another until the picture was merely a square frame with a blob of vague color in the middle. It looked like a framed version of the morning after the night before. Nevertheless, during the day session, I preferred to look at this when I was speaking rather than to look at the buzz of daily life going on down below, which only reminded me of my own lack of normality. I also became preoccupied with Mary's notes.

"You're not writing anything down about me, are you?" I'd ask her anxiously as she scrawled unintelligible notes down on paper. "They're not going to lock me up, are they?" I'd say over and over again.

Mary's strategy was very appropriate. We would enter her office. She would sit in her chair and say nothing, and I would mirror her until the silence became deafening. Then I would bombard her with a series of statements, posed as questions. She would mirror me, and my fears would bounce back off her at myself.

I would talk about myself. In the same clinical, matter-of-fact manner, I was able to relate some of the most horrific experiences of my past with very little feeling for these incidents at all. It was simple. So little of what had happened around me had actually reached me. Even when something had happened to my body, it was as though my body was either a mere object existing in "the world" or, at other times, a wall between "my world" within and "the world" outside.

Not surprisingly, in the recall of such events, I referred to myself as "you." This was because "you" logically captured my relationship to myself. One develops an "I" in interaction with "the world." Donna didn't interact; the characters did. Mary would try to get me to clarify whether I was implying that the events I was talking about applied to her, as she was the only "you" in the room. I tried to explain that this was how I described things. She continued. I reverted to using "I" in a conforming effort to avoid her pedantic emphasis on the pronouns I was using. Her efforts to get me to refer to these incidents in a personal manner overlooked the fact that my use of the word "you" captured the impersonal way in which I had experienced the incidents at the time they happened. She probably felt that she had to help me to overcome my depersonalization, as though this were some recently developed defense reaction. I don't think she realized that I had actually experienced life this way since the creation of Willie and Carol, and my subsequent ability to communicate through them, thirteen years before.

Every so often, Mary would trigger a reaction that wasn't experienced so objectively: fear of confinement, fear of rejection, fear of hopelessness, and fear of desertion. Such things were generally triggered by talking about the happy things: my grandparents, my father when I was small, and my little brother up until he was three. These fears, however, were not the cause of my problems, but the crippling result of my efforts after I began to participate in and try to reach out in "the world." Such fears had never, as I remember, caused my withdrawal and psychic retreat. I had done this even while I was with the few people who were honorary objects in "my world." My retreat was, most often, a response to that which tested my gentler emotions. I had no trouble with the coarser ones. Willie took care of those just fine. Bad feelings had no part in "my world."

I had a preoccupation with keeping control, as Mary saw it. I had been trying to get reassurances from her that I could reach out yet keep control at the same time. I was trying to reach her in order that she could reach me, but she stood her ground and tried to make me realize that this would have to be on her terms. What she didn't realize was that, in laying down such ground rules, she was giving me the message that my efforts to reach out weren't good enough. She seemed to be challenging me to compete on her level. I could only do so by being mentally detached from my emotions. We were both hitting brick walls.

I decided I would help her to reach me. I would give up some of the secrets that formed the strong foundations of "my world." It was as though I had gone to a summit and put forward a proposal for disarmament. Mary, in her protected role as the professional, had learned and leaned on the lessons of professional distance and was not going to come to the party. As she put it, "You came here to see me; I didn't come here to see you." This statement was meant for both our good, I suppose, so that I would not become too dependent or bring her down to my level, and so that she would be free of the personal assault often inflicted in the emotional turmoil of therapy.

My dependency on Mary, however, was the only way she was going to see the real me. The character of Willie thrived on distance. Carol could adjust to anything. Donna, however, could never reach out for a hand or ask for it. That hand simply had to be offered unconditionally on whatever terms it would take to bring Donna out of the darkness of the cupboard. Carol charmed and chatted. Willie explained, analyzed, and impressed. Donna lurked in the shadows waiting to see if Mary would find the key to the cupboard door.

IIII

AS FAR AS normality was concerned, though Carol and Willie could act relatively normal, Donna was actually closer along the continuum to normal. Crippled as hers were in "the world" only Donna had emotions that functioned in "her world."

Carol strutted in one day to give up the secret of Willie's existence. Willie always took things too seriously, pulling the plug on the good times and pulling everybody into line. Carol seemed to fall into line with the rest of them and, in the process, disappear. Carol kept the performances going, but Willie ran the theater as though it were a prison. Carol's charm, sociability, and cheerfulness simply couldn't co-exist with Willie's cutting criticisms of the self she portrayed. Her solution, as far as therapy was concerned, was simple: she wanted the good times back. She wanted her relationship with Chris back to how it was. Mary, though charmed by her social naïveté, found Carol's goals in need of development.

"I hear this voice over and over inside my head sometimes," said Carol, referring to Willie but not willing to give up the secret of who the voice belonged to or the feelings from which it originated. Mary asked what the voice was telling her. "It tells me, 'Don't tell them; they won't believe you,' " said Carol, testing the water.

Mary was intrigued, and together they discussed the possible origins of the message; Mary finally deciding that it was a memory of something my mother had said.

Of course it had been something my mother had said. The character of Willie had arisen from Donna's ability to mimic combined with her mother's ability to taunt and torture her into responding. As Willie, I had mimicked the words. Unable to acknowledge any communication, Willie had stored them and retrieved them as appropriate weaponry. Eventually, however, in frustration, these same weapons were used against the self from which this character had sprung. In an effort at autonomy, Willie had learned to resent Donna's vulnerability, the very quality he had been created to protect. Both Carol and Willie had progressed through the various stages of personality development and this could have helped to refine and shear off their rough edges had it not been for their fear of recognition, which developed as an antithesis within the same body. There is no operation for psychically connected, incompatible Siamese twins. Integration was the only real solution. Unfortunately, each character had his or her own solution.

Mary had written me out a prescription. It seemed to me that she had interpreted my predicament as schizophrenia. Naturally I was insulted. I had tried so hard to believe otherwise, yet I still feared that I was mad. Mary had unknowingly confirmed it.

My friend Robyn had said that people believed what they wanted to believe. Mary's behavior had exemplified this. Carol took the tablets randomly, abusing them as she would any other medication she was given. On top of about eight tablets she downed a quantity of Cognac, then called Mary's number at home.

Carol was losing awareness, and I felt the fear of hopelessness come over me, thinking that permanent damage might have been done; so ironic to have it happen at a time when I was getting help.

Mary answered the phone. She spoke to me casually and calmly. I found it hard to understand what she was saying, but my mind had latched on to an image as Mary described how she was playing chess with her cat, which was prancing about on the covers of her bed. My mind was replaying a similar image from a Shirley Temple movie. I was again back to three years old. My voice was switched to "automatic pilot" while my sense of self came over me in waves. It was as though I was flying through myself every so often. Yet I had had this experience before without the influence of drugs or alcohol. Through this, I was able to be myself with Mary more than I ever had before. Perhaps, like the television set years before, it was the distance of the telephone line that made it possible.

Mary took me off the tablets. The only jot of difference they had made was that I had become convinced that I could not trust Mary enough to give up the secrets that could have helped truly to undo some of the damage in a more permanent way. The strategy for "letting go" lay not in my reliving of the events that had gone on in "the world" around me, but in my giving up the defenses that had shielded me from the effects of these events. These defenses consisted of a book's worth of secrets steeped heavily in symbolism, as they came well before a time when they could be captured by words in any traditional sense.

Mary had obviously little grasp of the world I remembered so clearly before the invasion of touch and words and the expectation of participation. She set about helping me to tidy up the constructions that had been suffocatingly built upon faulty, undeveloped foundations. I was two years old, and she had never really seen me.

||||

I HAD BEEN working in a shop not very far from the hospital. The boss there had two daughters around my own age and was sexually harassing me. I found it hard to get along with anyone or serve customers but I managed to hold things together and get through each day. I had become attached to one customer, an old man who waved hello to me every day and who had become my new grandfather.

Perhaps in latching on to grandfather figures I was trying to continue in my emotional development where I had left off. Yet at the same time my grandfather had begun to die for me long before he actually passed away. I remember always believing that both he and my father had died when I was three.

They had both stopped being objects in my world when I

was three, but my father continued to live as one of many of the adults around me, and my grandfather didn't die until I was five, whereupon my grandmother left to live in the Australian bush.

I can actually remember trying to reach out for my grandfather with my eyes. It was in this sorrowful, unreachable state of longing that I had stood by his bed when he passed away. I guess it was the sort of state of being one might expect from a ghost who had come to visit but could not communicate.

The old man who used to come into the shop I worked in had waved and said hello; and, though I had looked straight at him, I hadn't seen him, and he thought I'd ignored him. He came into the shop to buy something later the same day and ignored me. "Hi," I said, in an effort to reach out. He left without saying a word.

I began to panic. My body was operating on automatic pilot as I began to lose sense of what was around me. The shop was a mess of confused color and noise. I looked at the people I was working with: strangers. I didn't know why I was there, and I had to get out. I grabbed for my bag and bolted out of the shop. The city street was a nightmare: moving walls of people, my feet surrounded by feet everywhere. I was running. I pushed through the swarm of people, the confusing noise of the city screaming in my ears. I had to get to somewhere safe. I had to get to somewhere familiar. Mary would help me. Mary was my only hope.

A tram moved in front of me. I shoved people aside like objects blocking my path and climbed onto it. A man walked down the center of the tram. He was saying words over and over. I couldn't understand him.

"Money," he had said. I tore open my purse and threw the coins that were in it at his intruding feet. I got up and ran to the door, banging furiously on it with my fist. I was trapped, nowhere to go, nowhere to run, nowhere to hide. I began to cry hysterically, the noise rising up in my own ears until I could hear nothing else. The door opened.

I jumped out and ran across two intersections, cars

Most of these photos were taken by my uncle (the one who was going to adopt me). He and his family moved to the country when I was about six, so there are not many photos of me after that.

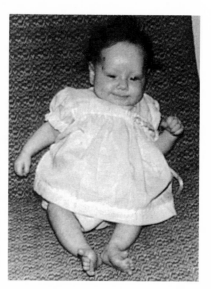

RIGHT: Here I am no more than a few months old. Even in this picture my eye contact isn't quite there. One eye stares blankly ahead and the other turns in (I used to do this later to put "the world" out of focus and thereby close it out—hard to tell if I was doing that here). My expression is, however, fairly divided, with one side animated and the other lost. Still, others may only see a little baby staring at nothing in particular.

RIGHT: This photo captures best how contented I was in "my world," as I stare obliviously through the camera.

LEFT: Taken moments after the previous photo, this one demonstrates the way my cognitive, emotional, and sensory shutdown happened—I am clearly stunned and rather "dead" in contrast to my brother. I have disappeared here, so to speak, and my brother clearly has no idea that I don't really know he exists.

ABOVE: This photo is typical of the sort of photo that usually comes with a blurb saying "psychotic." I think in this case, however, it is a good example of my intense commitment to getting lost in the spots (which are actually air particles I saw as foreground due to my visual hypersensitivity).

ABOVE: This shows, in contrast to my brother, how painful I found it to make direct eye contact.

Above: This is probably my favorite photo. Playing with my hair, and about as much of a "nobody nowhere" as a camera could capture, I am wearing the nightie I wore when I met the real Carol while swinging from my tree in the park. My brother, by the way, is in trouble for painting the shed door—I don't think you could find a less likely accomplice.

RIGHT: This shows the contrast between the way my brother and I related to the world: me holding on to my hair and my ball and looking off into nothingness, my brother relating directly to the person taking the photo.

ABOVE: This again shows my brother's interest in me and my preoccupation with a tactile, nonsocial world—as I said about the ballet dress, "Things, unlike people, were welcome to become a part of me."

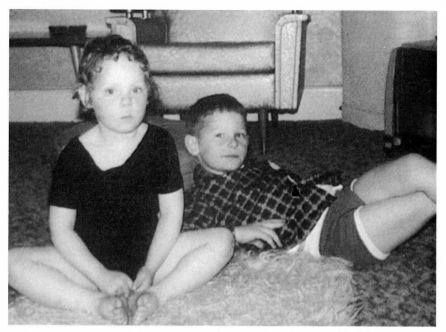

ABOVE: This photo could be entitled "Willie never made it as a ballerina." I may be looking through the camera, but the defensive expression is unmistakable. In contrast with earlier photos you can see the development of my brother's distance from, and lack of interest in, me.

LEFT: This was taken on my brother's sixth birthday. I am five here, and despite a balloon and my ball, I am clearly not able to be part of things. My brother's developing attitude speaks for itself.

ABOVE: Me (right) with my auntie and a cousin (not mentioned in the book), who lived in the house with the backyard where my grandmother died in a trailer. A good example of Carol in action, this captures Carol's "I laugh, you laugh, we laugh" response.

ABOVE: This is Willie, now having started school, aged about six. The look: pinched-up mouth, clenched fists, and glaring eyes—not relating terribly well to "the world."

ABOVE: What I see as Willie, aged twenty-one, having just secretly painted a "wisp" into the sign (hence the cheeky look).

RIGHT: Carol, at twenty-three, taken by David. You can see the fear in the tense, grimacelike smile.

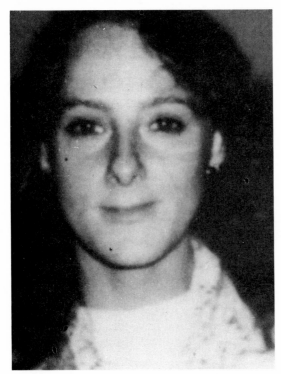

LEFT: Donna—me in "my world." It was taken after lunch with Bryn. I was twenty-two.

ABOVE: The shed wall, taken on a visit to my old house last year. You can still see where I wrote "Donna is a nut" in huge letters.

screeching, shouting assaulting my ears. A car had tapped me. I fell forward, momentarily sprawled across the hood.

The shininess of the hood stunned me. I lifted myself up with my forearms and looked at the two figures behind the glass of the windshield. They were pressed against the dashboard of their car, a look of shock upon their faces.

I had recognized one; he was the state political leader. I pointed at him, surprised at my recognition, and announced his name, like a scene from my first days at primary school: naming objects. That was my only moment of clarity as I rushed toward the doors of the hospital's psychiatric department.

||||

I HAD FORGOTTEN Mary's name. I had forgotten how to get upstairs to where she worked. I had forgotten how to speak.

I stood there at the reception desk in a state of panic, trying to articulate words and coming out with an unintelligible series of unconnected, half-articulated sounds that only heightened my panic. I began to cry and hyperventilate.

I felt I was going to drown in my own tears as I looked frantically into this receptionist's eyes, trying to pronounce Mary's name. She was a large, jolly-looking woman and reminded me of my friend Lina's mother. She remained patient, calm, and friendly as I stood there frantically choking on sounds. "M . . . Mar . . . M . . . Mary," I blurted out finally.

The woman got on the phone and called her down. Mary came downstairs and responded immediately to what she saw. She tried to put her arm around me. I edged away cautiously. She offered her hand. I followed her into the elevator, shooting glances back over my shoulder anxiously.

||||

WE ENTERED ANOTHER office. It was not her usual one. I was taken aback by the difference, but secure in her company. I sat without saying a word. She looked at me kindly, then reached into her bag and took out a sweet. My grandfather was back. I was three, and he hadn't yet lost me. I put the sweet cagily into my mouth as I sat across the room from Mary, like a rat in the corner. I began to smother a giggle caused by the secrecy of Mary having found her way into my world. "So, want to tell me what happened?" she asked with a rather calm, friendly yet concerned manner. I began to reply, then lost all sense of myself as Willie embarrassingly took the stage and tried to cover the tracks of how significant the events of the last half-hour had been.

"What happened to me?" Willie asked.

"You had what is called a panic attack," explained Mary. She asked me what had led up to it, and Willie told her that I didn't know. She helped me to retrace my steps, which Willie had been watching as an observer as Donna ran helplessly through the city streets.

Willie explained all the moves I had made. Mary pushed me to examine the personal significance of the old man. She was pushing me too far. I was discussing the events like some sort of newsreel commentator. The way I saw it, the old man was simply a friend who had upset me by snubbing me. Mary delved deeper, inquiring as to whether this had any personal significance for me. She was getting too close. There were simply some answers I was incapable of giving without losing control. Yes, he stood for my grandfather. The acknowledgment was made, and Donna sat there sobbing at the brutality and betrayal of the realization. She sat there sobbing and, because she could not be touched, there was no one to comfort her.

My grandfather's actual death had been discussed. No one mentioned the key to the real problem: that he, along with everyone else, had died when Donna was three, at the same time that Willie began to look into people's eyes with anger and Carol came through the mirror to keep them happy. If expectation had killed Donna, it was only because she was nowhere near ready to meet it, while her imaginary creations took on a life of their own and succeeded where she had failed. The real me was still hypnotized by colors at a time when Carol was learning to dance and Willie was learning to fight. It was as though I had died in "the world." Everyone had died when Donna disappeared, and nobody seemed to notice. In fact they thought she'd finally come to life.

Mary seemed to change her tack. It was as though she had decided that my problems were essentially social rather than simply psychological. We began to talk about the future. She asked me what I wanted to be. Antagonistically I replied that I wanted to be a "psychiatrist, just like you."

Mary and I continued to meet. She made me believe that nothing was impossible, and until then I had never tried to reach so high for the stars. Perhaps, to her mind, the sort of things I had been through had understandably made me unstable.

I was looking for the answers myself. Our conversations seemed to jump back and forth until we had reached some agreement that my lack of social awareness was due to my family.

My family's lack of social awareness and their inability to value many accepted social norms largely stemmed from their low socioeconomic status and their instability. Mary and I seemed to have agreed that most of my problems were due to the way in which people responded to me, which was an understandable deduction in view of the fact that I found most social contact hard to understand or respond to and that I saw the world very clearly in "them and us" terms.

||||

I DECIDED THAT I wanted to go back to school. I felt that if I could achieve my diploma I could get a job in a bank.

People in banks wore uniforms. People who wore uniforms were respected. I wanted to be respected. Therefore, I wanted to work in a bank. It didn't seem to make any difference that, at this stage, I had been giving away more money than the shops I'd been working in had been making or that I found it difficult even to add or subtract.

I had been seeing Mary for a year by this stage. I was now

eighteen years old. I had begun to fear the obviousness of my own instability, which became ever more noticeable and unforgivable with my increasing age. At times I felt I was in my twenties, at times I was sixteen at the most, and at other times I was still only three years old. I had been talking about this and had explained that I still was not ready to leave home, though it seemed I'd never had one. I had naïvely stated in a defeated tone that the problem these days was that no one wanted to adopt eighteen-year-olds. I looked up at Mary, who seemed to have tears in her eyes. I was touched that she was able to feel emotion for my words in a way I had never been able to. I responded to this with the respect I would have hoped for my own display of emotion. I said nothing and pretended not to notice.

The world was leaving me behind, and I knew it. The most blatant example of this was my unemployment, for I had by now been unemployed for two months and had to face the harsh reality that I was eighteen, unskilled, with an uneven work history and the same education as a fifteen-year-old, whom an employer could pay at almost half the adult rate. Chris was no help, and having no friends and no contact with any family members, Mary had become my whole world.

Mary helped me arrange an interview with the career adviser at an advanced education college near where I lived. I believed in her hopes for me and strutted through the college doors like I had found myself a new home.

"No," was the reply from the friendly man across the desk, he didn't think I had much chance of being admitted to school after having missed so many years. It was not that I'd been away from school for three years that mattered; it was my wanting to jump the two years I had not completed and go straight into the final high school year. I explained that there was no funding for students to return to secondary school and that, as I had no financial support from my family, I could not afford to make up the two years I had not completed.

It was suggested that I didn't necessarily have to tell anyone about my lack of education. It worked. All that was left was to pass an entry interview. I told the interviewer at the school that I'd been away from secondary school working and that I only wanted to jump one school year and said nothing of the two I'd missed. I explained that I had been to many high schools before I left, and that it might be hard to trace my records. I emphasized that I'd learned a lot since I'd left secondary school and asked if that shouldn't count for something. I must have done something right. I got a letter saying I could start. It was to cost forty dollars.

||||

MARY WAS OVER the moon for me. Chris didn't think it was a good idea. Basically Chris had been secure in the supposed superiority of our age difference and level of education.

Chris loved to laugh at the way I could be convinced of anything, like when he told me that all the sand at the beach was made by a machine. I had put some in my mouth and bitten into it at his instruction. "See," he said, "it's a special sort of plastic which is made by these really big machines." I was impressed. Armed with my newest piece of general knowledge, I went around showing off how much I knew and scoffing at the ignorance of all the people who never knew this before or didn't believe me.

Chris laughed under his breath all along, and it would sometimes be several months before he'd undo the damage. It wouldn't matter who told me the truth; the original teller had to change the story or I would remain confused and in doubt. Chris thought that my naïveté would change with education. When it came to this sort of naïveté, he was wrong.

Chris wasn't a complete opportunist. In some ways I think he did care about me. One time he met my father through his business and invited him back to the flat for a cup of tea.

It was awkward. I hadn't seen much of my father for a few years, except for the few times when I'd passed his work-place. Nor had I seen my mother. In the meantime my mother had not mentioned my existence to anyone who didn't know of me. To those who did, she got out of having to explain anything by enthusiastically telling them that I was a slut and a drug addict. Because I was not around to disprove it, this was eventually accepted by some, who showed sympathy toward her where before had been only blame and silence.

Here was my father sitting on my couch, in my living room, in my flat. He laughed and joked as though he accepted me exactly as I was and always had. He had such a good time that evening that he invited himself back.

My father and I had never really been allowed to talk to each other freely since I was about three years old. He had always been barked down by my mother, who jealously insisted that he should not "waffle back at me." It was assumed that anything I said as a child was not much more than mindless chatter, and my mother was not going to encourage this by letting someone talk to me on my own level.

My father's actions became his words—his laugh, the tone of his husky voice, the way he sang or whistled, and the way he would make objects speak. He would make the cats dance and sing. He would make a matchbox talk to a cigarette packet. When he came around to the flat, he hadn't changed. Chris had never really seen me like this. It made him feel even less important.

My father had never encouraged me to do anything, though he was enthusiastic about anything about which I was enthusiastic. I guess he was a bit like a cross between the real me and Carol. He made my return to school seem like an adventure, and I began to look forward to it, not just as an effort to be more like Mary and more acceptable to her, but also as though it was possibly "that special something" that was missing in my life. I decided that if my answers were to be found at school, then come hell or high water, I was going to find those answers, even if it killed me.

I had paid my forty dollars. I had selected the subjects— including biology and sociology—I had to take in order to take psychology. I was going to be like Mary. I had also decided to take music. English was compulsory.

||||

IT WAS MY first day. I was as pleased as Punch and looked the part, having taken great effort to look impressive. The only thing that was missing was a hanky pinned to my jacket.

I went to biology class. The teacher tried to test our knowledge by asking what we knew about how plants live. My hand was up in a shot. "They eat dirt and drink water," I said proudly. Everyone fell about laughing. They thought I was a comedian. I was deadly serious and didn't know what they were laughing about. The teacher asked one of the students to explain the process of photosynthesis. The student did this with ease. The teacher asked what happens to the plant's waste products. Unperturbed, my hand was up with all the urgency of a child about to wet itself. The teacher, wanting to be encouraging, acknowledged me. "They do it into the dirt," I said proudly. More laughs. "Not really," answered the teacher calmly, keeping a more or less straight face. He got someone else to explain. By this stage, I think people were unsure as to whether I was trying to be funny or whether I was a complete moron. To my way of reasoning, it was simple. I thought my answer was entirely logical and therefore must have been right. I was a bit bored by the prospect of having to learn other people's answers by heart.

||||

ENGLISH WAS DIFFERENT. There were no truly right or wrong answers. We were expected to read a lot of novels and poetry, and my long-winded yet evasive descriptions of what I had got out of what I'd read usually sufficed as some sort of excuse for an intellectual response that needed refinement in order to be understood.

English class was about the use of symbolism to convey

an impression. If there was anything I was good at, it was the ability to create pictures out of words to explain what might otherwise have been disjointed strings of black print on white paper.

In English I had something of an advantage in that I never read books thoroughly and had avoided getting weighed down in the useless little words, which seemed to steal away the story's meaning. The teacher was not looking for a blow-by-blow repetition of the books we reviewed, but an ability to capture the feel of them.

The books would be read out loud in class from cover to cover. Sometimes I'd watch and not listen. Sometimes I'd listen to the tone of the reader's voice in order to try to make out what he or she was understanding.

English class was also about creative writing. Enthusiastically I wrote my first piece of work, complete with the usual drawings over the words in order to capture the feel. The topic was to write about something that had happened to you. Naïvely, I wrote about the tragic events that had led to my first meeting with Mary. I had drawn tears over the pages.

"Donna, this is supposed to be a piece of personal writing," said the teacher.

"It is," I replied.

"Then who are you writing about?" she asked.

"Myself," I said confidently.

"Then, why have you referred to yourself as 'you' throughout the essay?" she asked. I didn't know why at the time.

"Is this meant to be a joke?" asked the teacher, referring to my essay.

"No," I replied, feeling a little bit hurt.

"What have you done with the periods and capital letters?" asked the teacher.

"I put them in," I replied innocently.

"Yes, but you've just put them in in any old place," she said.

"I put them in so the reader can get some breath," I replied with seeming logic.

"Are you serious?" she asked.

The teacher drew a series of sentences upon the blackboard to test my use of punctuation. "Put in the periods and capital letters," she commanded. I approached the words upon the blackboard and put in periods after every five or so letters, so that the reader could breathe. I then put capital letters on all the words in the sentence that were things, because these were names of things and all names had capital letters.

"I think you are going to need some remedial work," said the teacher, surprised and somewhat shocked.

"You gonna throw me out?" demanded Willie.

"No," said the teacher.

||||

I HAD BEEN looking forward to music. I thought I might have a chance to play a piano. But the activities in the classroom were very tightly controlled, and the piano was no exception.

There was no way around this. The piano was kept locked at all times. We were all told to choose an instrument we would like to learn. I wanted to play the piano, but was told that I couldn't because I didn't have one at home to practice on. When it came down to that, I didn't have one of anything to practice on.

Everyone was informed that they would have to pay for exams, which were required in order to pass the course. The cost of the exams was to be eight dollars each. It didn't take a genius to work out that someone who was not even earning enough money to pay her share of the rent could not afford the eight dollars a throw. I gave up music and took philosophy, though I had no idea what this was.

||||

I DID NOT last very long in philosophy. With the foulest look on my face, my fists clenched, my arms stiffly by my sides, I stormed out of the class after the first few days.

117

The teacher later asked me what the problem was. "They talk bloody Japanese in there," I said. "I can't understand a word they are saying." He assured me that if I came back to class he would try not to use "too many long words" and said he would not ask me any questions so that I wouldn't get embarrassed. I told him it was no use. He told me I would eventually get the hang of it. He reminded me of Mr. Reynolds. I decided to give philosophy another chance.

I eventually did learn a lot of big words, and it was also a very free class where there were really no right or wrong answers, so I didn't find it too embarrassing.

The point of the class was to discuss the beliefs of certain people, like Jesus Christ, among others. I found it interesting to hear what people believed in. It was a bit like eavesdropping. The way that people criticized the ideas of famous people who were not there to stand up for themselves brought out Willie's protective streak, and he began to argue against anyone who tried to make a point. The only problem was that when people would challenge me about what Willie personally believed, he would be completely at a loss. Willie had learned to argue for any side but still believed in none. For me, it was all a word game, but it was fun. Besides, my teacher liked me, and it was like having Mr. Reynolds back all over again.

||||

SOCIOLOGY WAS ALL about the effect of family, education, and social class on making a person who they are. Well, Mary was not a sociologist, but this seemed to be similar to what she believed. The last year of therapy had taught me a lot about analyzing such things, as well as about breaking down therapy into a system. I then used this system to try to understand the analyzer so I could work out how to be like her.

The idea of social class became my primary, more impersonal way of accounting for my feelings of "them" and "us." In part Mary had helped me to interpret things this way, which was a quite natural yet subjective way of making sense of my feeling of not belonging in "the world." I certainly found it too frightening to own up to the secrets of what "my world" versus "the world" really meant, even to myself. I jumped at the opportunity to examine my dilemma by analyzing something similar to, yet removed from, the real situation.

Mary was my mirror. Mary came from a different class background. Therefore, the fact that she felt a sense of belonging and I didn't must have been due to this. The fact that she did not dismiss the idea made it true.

||||

MOST OF ALL, I lived for psychology. Though my teacher was as hard as nails, I felt that she had some sort of respect for the effort I was making.

A lot of psychology had to do with finding out how things worked. The subject of the mind was, for me, like the study of an object that worked according to a system. Systems were relatively predictable, the sort of thing that came with guarantees. I could respect this sort of knowledge.

The textbook had a lot of pictures and diagrams, which made the rest of the text easy to follow. There were lists of big psychological terms to be memorized, and all of it would add to my ability to take myself apart and put myself back together.

I had discovered that my mind, too, was a system. If I understood it, then that was a form of protection. I could learn to explain why I was the way I was. I could work out whether I was in fact mad or stupid, and I could explain it as though I were that very symbol of intelligence and sanity I so looked up to—my psychiatrist.

Nevertheless, I was not like Mary. My language was filthy, coarse, and uncontrolled. My manners were almost nonexistent. I took everything extremely literally. And I handed my work in on reused paper.

The psychology teacher handed back our work. She had

marked it purely on content rather than on presentation. She got to mine and announced that she had to give me the highest mark in the class even though she had never had to read from so disgusting a piece of paper. I had used white typing fluid to go over an entire page of previous work before writing my new work on it and handing it in. I was poor, it was true, but it never occurred to me that the whitener probably cost more than the paper I had used it on.

IIII

MY BIOLOGY TEACHER found out that I could not add or subtract. I had been confused by my earlier high school teacher who had asked me to show all of my working-out on paper. I had my own system up until then, which had worked just fine. When I couldn't learn theirs, I had also assumed that, although correct, if I couldn't show my calculations, then my system was no good, either. As I had never learned their system, I continued unsuccessfully to try to use it, never reverting to my own logic.

The biology teacher suggested that I use the calculator. I didn't know how. He tried to show me how it worked. When he asked me to work out a percentage of something, I tried to find the "of" button and gave up, furious and frustrated. My teacher realized I had big problems.

My remedial math teacher was a dream. She was not at all like a teacher. She had plaited blond hair and reminded me of Elizabeth, the girl at the special school fifteen years earlier, whose hair I'd reached out to touch.

I watched her work things out on paper. A smile would break out across my face. "That's great," I'd say. "Can you show me how you did that trick?" She would try to explain that math was not a series of magic tricks, and I would sit there trying hard to believe her.

There were some things I could work out just fine, but, unlike mathematics in school, I could not say how I reached the answers. Eventually, however, she helped me to learn a reasonable amount of math. She was very proud of me, and I was very proud of myself.

||||

MARY WAS VERY proud of me, too. I still went and saw her every week, but our sessions were progressively becoming more social than strictly professional. I wonder if she realized that it was this acceptance that raised my self-esteem and motivated and inspired me more than anything else.

There was not really so much to be gained by my learning to be more social with people in general, as I continued to close most of them out and most of them continued to find me weird.

I had reached out to Mary as somebody I could trust in "the world." She had accepted me as more than a patient; she had accepted me personally. I had become attached to her in my own distant way. In my mind she had become Carol's long-awaited mythical mother. Yet, as all relationships existed within me rather than between myself and others, there was only one way to bring this attachment inescapably into my own world. Willie compulsively set about becoming like this person who symbolized protection, strength, and self-control.

I was swinging from one extreme to the other, as both Carol and Willie were each other's antithesis. Yet as the trapeze swung ever higher, and each horizon broadened with my new experiences, I began to catch glimpses of my true self.

||||

I MANAGED TO find myself another flat, despite the fact that I had only two cleaning jobs to support myself with. I had no bed. I had a couch and a coffee table from the Salvation Army, but I had left Chris with almost everything else.

One of my neighbors gave me an old radio that made a loud hum. This became my best friend.

I was earning twenty dollars a week; the rent on the flat was thirty-five. I was living on a wish and a prayer when a part-time job I had applied for came through just in time.

I cycled down to my new job in the takeaway food shop almost every night after school. I ate the scraps that were left over at the end of each night, and nobody knew that this, and the meals my old friend Robyn was supplying, was the only food I had to eat.

Cheryl, one of the girls I worked with, caught on and, against the establishment's regulations, began to sneak food into the bottom of my usual take-home cardboard lunch box full of chips. She would fill up this box with chips for me each night. One night I got to the bottom of the box and found pieces of warm roast chicken. I cried.

My father started coming around. I was grateful for the company. He would take me out shopping. I would buy my usual packets of jelly and a packet of rice. He would try to impress the cashiers with the amount of money he spent on groceries. He even bought chocolate biscuits for his dog. I paid for my own shopping. He didn't seem to notice my poverty, and I never drew his attention to it.

One day I dreamily suggested that he loan me the deposit on a flat I'd seen in an advertisement. I would pay the weekly installments so that I would never again be home-less. The deposit was four thousand dollars. "I'd love to," he said, "but I'd never have that kind of money." The next week he told me how he had just given my mother four thousand dollars to cover the cost of switching places be-tween her bathtub and toilet, putting special mirrored tiles on the bathroom wall, carpeting the bathroom floor, and changing the stainless steel taps for gold-plated ones.

If learning had made me able to see such cruelty and in-justice for the first time, I wondered if it was really worth it. Then I thought of Mary and told myself that I would be like her, and never so inhuman and materialistic as this.

||||

I HAD PASSED the school year with average to high marks. It was an incredible feeling, and Mary and I were both quite over the moon about it. But with the enthusiasm came the fear of it all ending.

My structured life of relative consistency was coming to an end. I felt like I was drowning in the uncertainty of the future.

In the midst of the glamour of celebrations on the last day of school, I stood alone, as always, watching people talking with one another. I had not made many friends among the students and had spent most of my spare time either alone in the cafeteria or up in the atmosphere of the college counseling service, where I felt so at home.

A student from my class approached me and surprisingly asked me for my address.

I had taken on my class as I had taken on my family: a one-woman war against the masses I vaguely termed "them." In turn I had been shunned, and even worse, some had approached me on their own but apologized that they couldn't speak to me in front of their friends, who thought I was mad. Yet this girl had blatantly walked away from her group of friends to approach me. She gave me her address. I gave her mine.

At Christmastime I received a card from this girl. She said that, although she had never been close to me, she had been inspired by me and had learned a lot about life by the courage and endurance she had seen me display. She felt guilty for having had a privileged life and wrote that she had decided to become a nurse. Tears came to my eyes as I read this, alone in my empty flat at Christmas. It was the first time I realized that I had inspired anybody, though I had done so not through courage but through the dual motivations of hope and fear.

||||

I HAD STOPPED seeing Mary on a professional basis. I had come such a long way since that first day I had come into the hospital in pieces, mentally, emotionally, and physically.

Our therapy sessions had become coffee sessions. More to the point, they had become too personal to continue on a purely professional level. We had decided to stay in touch, and for once in my life, I kept to that promise.

It was now possible for me to don that uniform I had dreamed of and walk into a bank teller's position. My math, though much improved, was still not up to scratch. It wasn't this, however, that changed my mind. I had come further than to still believe so simplistically that wearing a uniform would bring me the respect I had so wanted as the foul-mouthed little girl who worked in a factory.

I had survived a year with virtually no income, and my marks qualified me for entry to a university. There I would be eligible for a tertiary education allowance, which ironically was not available at the time for the secondary level. I decided to go to a university.

IIII

IN SOME WAYS Mary had been right. My naïveté, and the way it left me floundering socially, had been compounded by my lack of education. On the other hand, my lack of education had served as a good excuse for it.

The more educated I became and the wider the social group I mixed in, the more I came to be seen as an eccentric and comic figure when my newfound sophistication would slip and I'd do or say something far more representative of a fool then of a scholar. I still had a few advantages. I was only nineteen years old, and I could always blame it on my class background.

I had two months to wait until the beginning of the university term. I had applied for several courses, including youth work, social work, welfare, arts, and interior design.

The caring professions appealed to that part of me that already had a strong protective instinct and had come to mirror Mary. Arts appealed to the indecisive part of me that could not tie itself down to any particular choice of subject. The subject that was probably closest to my truest nature was the one I took least seriously: interior design. This appealed to that same part of me that had created miniature worlds in the special school sixteen years before. This was the part of me that loved to organize things according to shape, color, and pattern, and fell in love with the things in people's homes far more than I fell for the people themselves. As always, in the end, this part of me lost out and the other two struck a compromise. I took the arts degree and transferred during my second year to the School of Social Sciences.

||||

FINANCING MY STUDIES didn't seem like it was going to be too much of a problem. At this stage, fees had not been introduced and the education allowance seemed only to be a matter of sending in a form. I was wrong. It took six months for the first payment to come through.

My job at the takeaway shop had been cut back, and I could no longer afford my flat. It was three days before New Year's Eve, and I was homeless. I had tried place after place to get a room in a shared house. Finally some people took pity on me and called me back as I walked away dejected from yet another attempt to get a room.

I spent New Year's Eve alone in the darkness of this new home. I played a Bette Midler record called "Friends" and cried at my inability to sustain any real sense of belonging or attachment, and thought about the many well-meaning people I had walked away from time and time again.

Finally I called up my family. My mother was partying, and strangers kept grabbing the phone and drunkenly wishing me a Happy New Year. I could hear the music in the background and imagined people dancing and laughing. I wondered what it would be like to be there. I tried to imagine what it might have felt like if I could just once have felt like part of things. I hung up and counted the seconds to midnight. "Happy New Year, Donna," I said to myself. I burned a candle and, watching it, fell asleep.

||||

THE UNIVERSITY TERM began, and I tried desperately to get lost in it all.

I had chosen linguistics and philosophy on the basis of

having walked down the hallway and asked someone what the subject was, if it was good, and if I should take it. I also took sociology, in pursuit of my goal of becoming like Mary.

I was completely lost. The place was far too big, with too many walls, too many people, and too many fluorescent lights. I went around everywhere turning them off. When I didn't, they made me fall asleep.

I slept in the middle of my philosophy classes. When I wasn't sleeping with my eyes closed, I slept with them open. Eventually the teacher had said I was quite simply "scatty." I had tried to explain that I couldn't follow the class time-table, that I couldn't understand the instructions set out in the handbook, and that I couldn't get anything but words out of what I was reading. The head of the department called me "a complete and utter moron."

I enjoyed linguistics. Linguistics took language apart and put it back together. It showed how all language can be broken down into different types of systems. The class was a series of diagrams and cycles. I took to this like a duck to water.

In sociology I tried so hard to do well that I tied myself up in knots. I tried to write and wound up giving the teacher a handful of evasive, jargon-laden, disjointed sentences.

I was sent off to remedial English. The problem, however, was simply that expressing my own opinion and beliefs—expressing what I felt—was simply too threatening. "Evasive," "impersonal," and "disjointed" captured how I found things very accurately.

Socially nothing had changed. As always, I had made few friends, and things remained this way for two years. Carol found it very hard to attend classes, but Willie was a born scholar.

The wait for my allowance had one saving grace. I had, with the back payments of my allowance, bought myself an old piano. I learned to love and live for the time spent with my piano. I began to write music straight away. I could mimic other people's music with relative ease, but I learned truly to express my feelings through the creation and playing of my own music. At first I wrote classical music. I could not read sheet music, so I could not as yet write my music down on paper properly. I had simply to remember my pieces, which usually sufficed. As these pieces became more complex, I developed a strategy of writing down timing using a series of dots and dashes of differing lengths, and learned to write the pitch over these dots and dashes using their letter names and arrows showing whether they went up or down in pitch. Eventually I brought home some music theory books and taught myself a bit about standard notation, though largely I still relied upon my own system.

Through my music I began more and more to reach and express my true self. My music spoke of the things I loved, of the wind and the rain, of freedom and hope, of happiness in simplicity, and of triumph over confusion. However, the closer I came to bringing myself out, the greater became the fears, which caused serious conflicts between my inner self and the characters I used to communicate with the outside world.

IIII

I BEGAN TO have night terrors again.

I got up and went into the bathroom in a sort of dream state. I caught a glimpse of the hallway light shining under the closed door of the flat. It triggered something, and I felt myself falling, losing a grip on any sense of the true reality around me.

Like the day I had run out on my job and made my way to the hospital, I again forgot where I was or why I was there. Terror swept over me. I was on my hands and knees whimpering like a baby. I felt the coldness and hardness of the tiles and looked at my hands sprawled out on them.

I couldn't breathe. I felt the fear of the unknown, which lurked somewhere in the same room. I whimpered, terrified, lost, and helpless. I curled up, shaking with fear, and rocked like a baby. I tried to speak but I couldn't find how to. I cried myself back to sleep.

This disturbed me profoundly. I had been through two years of therapy only to find that I was still vulnerable to these ghostly reminders of a self that had been buried long ago but refused to die.

I phoned Mary. I told her that I felt there were obviously some things that I still hadn't sorted out. I felt that these things lay somewhere in my past and it was time I began to unbury them.

I went around to my mother's house and climbed in through the laundry window. I sat in the big empty house; the ghosts of the past that had haunted me through so many nightmares seemed to sit around the table with me.

The door opened. Voices entered. Not surprised at my behavior, but at my presence, family members sat down. Willie glared at my mother hatefully, demanding answers.

IIII

I WENT TO see the doctors who had seen me as a child. I wanted to hear what was on my medical records. I also went to the primary school I had attended and stood at the foot of the tiny staircase that led to the Psych and Guidance room —an attic that the school now no longer used. I visited my first high school, from which I had disappeared on my trip to the country. Finally I went to see an aunt who had been a regular visitor to the house during my early childhood.

My aunty was surprised to see me. It was the first time I'd visited her in about six years. She had always been very fond of me.

I told her that I had found out that my birth certificate was not a copy of the original; that it was a "second schedule" and that the registrar had told me to go and ask my parents to give me the answers to why this was so. I felt that here was a good place to start.

I had once been told that my aunty's little girl had overheard a conversation between her parents about how I could have been her sister. I told my aunty that the adoption agency had identified my certificate as an adoption certifi-

cate, and I wanted to know why. I grilled her for the answers.

My aunty told me the story behind my mother's never-
ending threats to put me in a children's home. My aunty and
my uncle had discussed the possibility of adopting me. I
had, however, been put into my grandparents' care by my
father, and as my grandparents lived in a shack in our backyard, I remained at home. Upon the death of my grandmother, my parents once again became my full custodians.

I looked at my aunty and wondered what it might have
been like growing up with her, with a little sister instead of
a little brother. Still, I wouldn't have swapped my early experiences with my little brother for the world.

My aunty was cornered. She told me everything she could
remember from the moment I was born.

When it came to everything that was wrong with me—my
not speaking to people, my aversion to closeness, my preoccupation with the unreachable world within my own mind
—to her it was simple: my mother had caused it.

There was much that justified this opinion, but Willie examined what she said from an objective observer's point of
view.

I had not linked the tragedy of what she had seen with
the pleasant, beautiful, and hypnotic experiences of mere
color, sensation, and sound that had held me spellbound
until I was about three and a half. I had been unaware of the
pain of sores from unchanged diapers or my mother's neglect or brutality until I began to become aware of people's
efforts at getting my attention.

The hypnotic fascination I had for the spots in the air left
me with very little sensation of my own body except for the
shock and repulsion of the invasion of physical closeness.
Even the comfort I derived from being picked up by my
grandmother was found, not in snuggling up to her, but in
holding on to the chain around her neck or enmeshing my
fingers in her crocheted cardigan.

There was something overwhelming about giving in to
physical touch. It was the threat of losing all sense of sepa-

rateness between myself and the other person. Like being eaten up, or drowned by a tidal wave, fear of touch was the same as fear of death.

My aunty had recalled many memories of my early childhood, but none had really struck a chord. Willie stood there remembering many of these, but did so without any feeling for the self who had experienced them. Then, as my aunty recalled an event when I was three, it triggered something, and my mind replayed it in all its vividness and horror.

I was back there. I could see my aunty across the room. I could hear the pleading tone in her voice and sensed danger. I was watching everything around me happen as though in slow motion, though still moving far too fast for me to be able to respond in time.

I looked up at the figure of my mother. I shot silent glances in the direction of the pleading voice from across the room. I looked down at the opened tin of cold spaghetti in front of me and was aware of the fork in my hand.

I had not heard the introduction: the threat of death against my spilling a single drop of food. I never connected the repeated slapping with the event. It was just something that came to me from out of the blue as a series of shocks.

I felt the dishcloth being forced into my mouth. It made me gag. I was choking as I vomited up against it.

The pleading voice was at war with the cutting snarl of my mother's voice. I glanced at the black and white striped cord as though it was a snake. It began to whip my face. I could not cry, or speak, or scream. I looked at my aunty and collapsed on the cold smooth surface of the table in front of me and vomited through my nose. I thought I had drowned.

Willie stood there back in the present, with the sound of my aunty's sobs begging me not to make her tell any more.

There was a rising choke of vomit in my throat and a deafening scream inside my head that couldn't get out. Willie glared at my aunty, and the stifled tears had not even made it to his eyes. In a calm, hard, and stilted voice Willie had asked why she had done nothing.

Without waiting for a reply, I went wandering down the hallway of my aunty's house like an automaton.

My cousin's room branched off to one side. I looked through the door. My cousin had been given the furniture from my old room as a child. There on my old bed was the same bedspread, white with fine yellow flowers embroidered on it.

The bed was white and curved and smooth, and I could remember tracing its shape with my hand over and over. I could remember biting into the wood and feeling it give way with a fine crackling sound as the paint chipped away. Against another wall was the matching dressing table. Its three folding mirrors seemed to have captured the ghost of Carol, who had stood in front of it many times, whispering the name Donna and trying to feel it.

The mirror seemed to call me. I approached it and looked deeply into the eyes of the girl looking back. Willie was gone.

Against the other wall was the wardrobe—the wardrobe in which Carol had left me behind. I held my breath in front of it. I ran my fingers along the pattern of the wardrobe door's handle. I was afraid and felt as though I was being swept up in a sort of magic. The magic of childhood. I opened the door and got in. In the darkness, closing the door behind me, I sat down and curled up in a ball.

After awhile I got out of the cupboard and left the room in a hurry. I left my aunty's house like a cornered rat that had suddenly found a way out. I had begun to touch upon the answers to what was missing. I went home, curled up in a ball, and rocked for three days.

||||

I HAD MOVED in order to live up-country, an hour's drive each way from the university. I enjoyed the drive every day, often getting lost as the road went around one bend after another. I often arrived and knew only that I had driven by the fact that my hands were on the steering wheel when I stopped.

The country was absolutely delightful, with the smell of the rain on the wind and the feel of dirt, grass, and dead leaves beneath my feet. I had cats, and I had a vegetable garden and a special place to put my piano.

The place I shared sat at the foot of a small mountain. A mountain stream trickled over a steep path of naturally multicolored pebbles. There were trees everywhere, and each seemed to have its own personality. The mountain stream ran down into a creek, which ran directly past the back of this house. I'd cross the creek and throw pebbles onto the opposite bank, creating an island, then go and sit upon it, safe, untouchable, and alone.

||||

I WAS TWENTY-ONE. My older brother had invited me to his new home as a special gesture on my birthday. I had insisted that my mother not be there. This agreed, I consented to go.

My father and younger brother were there, yet it was as though they were miles away. The atmosphere was strained and eerie.

My younger brother felt like a complete stranger. Looking at his almost adult body, I was disturbed by his presence and could not recognize him as my brother, though my logic persisted in telling me he was.

My father was tense and distant. He was performing with all the fervor of a circus clown, trying to keep the atmosphere light. My older brother and I threw cutting remarks across the table at one another as Willie celebrated my twenty-first birthday.

Not unexpectedly, the whole evening came to blows. Willie was trouble looking for a place to happen, and as usual, he got it. Willie looked at the strangers surrounding me and knew that the sense of belonging that evaded me would not be found here.

||||

I BEGAN TO think a lot about my grandfather. I began to wonder what had happened to me that had caused him to die in "my world" two years before he had passed away in "the world." I decided to go to the cemetery for a visit.

I sat upon his grave. I had not visited it for eleven years. I remembered how we had gone to visit it when Tom was three. My father had told Tom that Pop lived in there under the ground. Tom had tried to find a way into the grave and became frustrated and angry that we were not able to go in.

A leaf tumbled upon the wind across the grave and landed up against my body. I picked it up and said: "Thanks."

On the way home I pulled into an isolated service station in a semirural suburb. A goat began to nibble at my tire. I asked the attendant if the goat would do it any harm. He replied that he was going to do harm to the goat and said that he was going to shoot the goat that night. "No, you're not," I said boldly. "I'll take him home with me." The attendant was happy to let me have him.

On the way home I began to cry. My vision was a blur as I watched the road in front of me through a blanket of tears. After sixteen years it had suddenly occurred to me that my grandfather had not deliberately intended to die. I named the goat after my grandfather.

||||

I FELT RELATIVELY at home living in the house in the country, and the long drive to school each day gave me time to dream and think. Yet I still hadn't found the mythical sense of home that seemed to evade me. I awoke one day from a dream that told me I was not going to stay where I was.

I had dreamed of a dark-haired young man. Though I had never met him in my waking life, I knew his name, his family background, the sort of person he was, and his way of life. He and I had a great friendship, the likes of which I had never had with any man I'd so far lived with.

In the dream I had been sharing a house with this man but was now sharing a house with a woman who, curiously, I recognized as an acquaintance I had met through my friend

Stella when I was fourteen. In the dream this woman and I became best friends.

I dreamed that it was again my birthday. The three of us stood around a dining table that was draped in an antique lace tablecloth. We had all raised our glasses (crystal glasses I had later been given by a friend). "Happy Birthday," these two had said.

I told a friend about the dream in detail. "Looks like I'm leaving," I had said. Two years later the dream came true, exactly as I had seen and described, down to the last detail.

||||

I WAS NOW in my third year at the university. I had learned to make sense of sociology in terms of my own experiences. I had dropped philosophy and began to choose subjects that were more closely aligned to the areas in which I thought I might find the answers I was looking for. I had left behind my compulsion to become like Mary in the face of something even more valuable. I had begun to try to find out about myself.

I had become known for my strangely detached and outspoken viewpoints on the usefulness or lack thereof of what I was learning. I had begun to earn popularity as myself to an extent.

Each side of me had begun to become more closely aligned to my true self, though they were still miles apart from one another. It was as though they were all one continuum and my real self was kept protected, unexpressed, within the middle. At their extremes, the characters I had become had denied my existence and lost awareness of me. At other times, they were depersonalized, communicative, worldly versions of myself that were able to sound out people and environments for a self that could not cope with things of such complexity.

If my true self was merely my subconscious, then by some tragedy it hadn't completely gone to sleep. If it were my conscious mind, then it was like a waking dream state that had not truly woken up. The depth of the feeling I felt as myself made all else feel empty, manufactured, and two-dimensional by comparison. The world these two communicative versions of myself endured was, to me, a complexity of confusing and invasive inflictions. Thus, everything my characters created had to be torn apart in my effort to break free. Carol's friendships were torn apart and discarded. Willie's strong ideas were constantly turned on their head and discarded—always at the point at which they were held so dogmatically.

Life behind glass. Living death made tolerable.
Pure fear of the one touching touch,
Which could smash the glass forever,
And send the dancer plummeting from her tightrope,
Into the knowing of the unknown.
Today it seemed the world was a scene
In a book of secrets from which we tore a page.
A touching touch shattered the glass between two worlds,
And the cold wind of uncertainty whistled a chill
Through body and soul, entwined for the first time,
Like vines wild and free.

Bryn was unusual. He stood out from the crowd. He was quiet and solitary, but there was something more, something quite different. Other people would speak to me when they wanted to get to know me. Bryn would simply come and exist within my company. Bryn was able to communicate but was very hard to reach through the usual kind of communication. He had sensed a differentness about me, too. As we clicked, the rest of the world around us disappeared.

Never, since the girl I had met in the park when I was three, had anyone been able to capture me so totally. I was either in Bryn's world or he was in mine. Perhaps we existed in a world altogether different, and until now, I had never found any other person who existed in it, too.

Bryn and I simply found ourselves in the same places. We

could not say what we felt; we merely sensed it, and, in the style that the respect for distance called for, we said nothing.

In fact Bryn and I communicated very little at all. We communicated via our discussion of nature and the things around us, poems we had read or written, and films we had seen. We never discussed what the significance of any of these things may have been for each other. In fact we spoke to ourselves about such things far more than to each other, and simply allowed the other person the privilege of listening in.

I began to brush Bryn's hair. He bought me lunch, and we shared the food on the grass, beneath a special tree. We both found it extremely difficult to look into each other's eyes, and when we did it was again the frightening feeling of losing oneself.

People said we were in love with each other. I defensively told them not to degrade what I had with Bryn by any comparison with a usual sort of relationship.

During the year I had grown so close to Bryn, I had never lost my fear and absolute nervousness at seeing him. Sometimes this had made seeing him a torture almost impossible to tolerate. I stuttered and shook much of the time. Because he was like me, he had all the right responses and merely looked into space, never letting it register that he noticed. Basically such things did not matter, and it was this simple unconditional acceptance that meant that in each other's company we were not "being there for each other"; we were simply "being."

There was no desperateness to reach out and touch each other in "the real world." The only thing that mattered was that someone had been able to touch me emotionally within "my world."

One day we silently and without any deliberateness touched hands. I was terrified. The pain of this emotionally touching touch was almost more than I could bear. We sat side by side, ignoring the fact our hands were touching, and allowed ourselves to experience the feeling. I felt as though I was going to die.

llll

I WAS GIVING a girl from the university a lift home. As we drove past the special school I had been to as a small child I pointed out that I had gone there.

"You couldn't have," she said. "That's a special school."

"What do you mean?" I asked her.

"It's a school for special-needs children," she explained. "My mother works there as a speech therapist."

"It must have changed," I said naïvely.

"No, it's always been a special school," she said. "You can ask my mother."

Bryn and I lay stretched out on the grass. I told him what this girl had said. "I went to a special school, too," Bryn confided. "I had been sent away because my parents thought I was mad," he said. He told me how he spent time in the "home" and that he had had trouble communicating with people. His parents had thought that he might have been schizophrenic.

Bryn didn't have delusions about the people around him. He did, however, often feel painfully uncomfortable with them. Bryn was not tortured by hallucinations, only by his communication problems and his fear of emotional contact, which he had been able to handle almost better than me. If Bryn was schizophrenic, then I must have been so, too.

The thought was frightening; yet, from what I had read of schizophrenia, I didn't fit the description of symptoms terribly well. Though I feared closeness and felt people were invasive, these weren't deluded or paranoid feelings. Though objects were sometimes reduced to their more simplistic characteristics—color, sound, sensation—I never felt threatened by this.

Though I behaved wildly at times, or with complete complacency at others, it was not a matter of delusion; it stemmed from a shock reaction triggered by any type of closeness, from physical proximity to the mental closeness of understanding.

I had trouble with words, but this wasn't due to disordered thinking, and I never jumbled them up like a tossed salad. I either spoke them as emotionlessly mimicked repetitions of what other people had said, used a strange accent, stuttered, or found myself unable mentally to form the words to speak at all. All of these problems were due to fear of the overwhelming intensity of my very untouched emotions.

I had wanted to communicate and had created personas with which I could communicate and relieve some of my frustration and try to prove my intelligence and sanity. These, however, were not mythical monsters; they were the family I had created for myself within my insular and extremely lonely unreachable world. They served as translators to overcome the communication problems between "the world" and "my world."

I felt as though a ghost were watching me as I allowed people to play to my characters, to which I'd respond accordingly. It was more like an out-of-body experience. This had been happening for so long that, as an actress in my body, in a state of automation, I had lost sight of the controls that could bring me back down to earth. Mine were extreme versions of experiences of many people and didn't seem specific to schizophrenics.

||||

I TELEPHONED MY father.

"Why was I sent to that special school?" I demanded.

"What special school?" he said evasively.

"You know what I'm talking about," I said, and named the school to help jog his memory.

"Oh, that school," he said in sudden realization. I explained what I had been told by the girl whose mother worked there.

"What was wrong with me?" I demanded. "Was I mad?"

"No, listen," he said, "you were a little bit funny when you were small, but that was your mother's fault. There's nothing wrong with you."

"But what was I like?" I pleaded. "Please, I don't blame anyone. I really need to know. What was I like?"

"They thought you were autistic," my father said.

I asked him why.

"Well, you wouldn't let anyone come near you and you talked a bit funny. You used to go round saying what everyone else said all the time. But it's no wonder. Your mother used to hit you and shout at you all the time. No one listened to the things you said," he explained defeatedly. I thanked him.

I didn't know what "autistic" really meant. I simply thought it meant withdrawn. So! I was withdrawn. So what? I knew that all along. I knew the problems I had with being touched, with people saying kind things to me or wanting to get to know me. I knew, from my mother, that for a long time I had only repeated the things other people said. I still did not understand the way that this had affected so many other things in my life. I decided that I must have been mad, and buried my head in psychology books in order to find out just what it was exactly that I was afflicted with. None of these books made reference to autism, and I remained, as before, in the dark.

I moved back to the city, into the backyard of a shared house, where I lived in a trailer I had bought for myself. My piano lived inside the house. I lived out in the back garden with my two cats; I had left my goat where he belonged, in the mountains.

I spent all of my spare time writing music, and I had now begun to write songs, which began with the inspiration of knowing Bryn. When I wasn't writing music, I was buried in books on social psychology.

I had been forced to close myself off from Bryn. Unlike the relationships with other people I'd terminated in my life, he hadn't stopped existing. I simply felt too real in his company and felt I had to run away. For me this was a clear distinction. There were some people I left; there were others I ran away from. Problems arose for me when the people I left tried to hold on to me because they thought I was running away, and the few I ever ran away from saw me as merely leaving them and felt rejected and discarded. These seemingly subtle differences arose from striking differences in the emotions I felt at the time—all or nothing.

I retreated very strongly into feeling nothing again. The fight to regain and hold on to my true self had now reversed itself. I was not leaving; I was running.

Carol took the stage with a vengeance. This time my character was positively manic. Life became a constant barrage of nonstop parties and laughter and dancing and people. Willie sat in the director's chair. Carol turned back the hands of time and was now playing the part of the perpetual teenager.

||||

I BEGAN TO spend a lot of time socializing at the university.

Tim lived on campus. When I was first introduced to him I casually waved hello and couldn't have given two hoots about him one way or the other. He was tall and dark, and was studying medicine, as had his parents. He wasn't terribly impressed by me, either. We simply went on coexisting. I had not yet realized that he was the man I'd seen two years before in my dream.

Tim was into music; so was I. Somehow I had actually forgotten that I lived in a trailer in the backyard of that shared house with a piano of my own at home. I began to spend a lot of time playing the piano in the university music room.

||||

TIM AND I found each other listening to one another's music. Tim didn't write very much but played beautifully. Carol gave him the right to hear the songs and music that Donna was never sociable enough to play. Tim loved the songs and had a beautiful voice. He took the songs out of the shadows of Donna's world, where they had been shared with no one, and brought them out into the light. Carol sang along.

140

Tim loved the songs as though they were his own and began to relate to Carol through the music. Somehow Tim triggered another "on" button, and Donna began to emerge, not wanting to sing the songs anymore and wanting to take the music away from him.

At the same time as I resented him singing my songs, Tim was able to captivate me with his splendid ability to play my music almost as well as I had heard it within my mind at the time of writing it. In my mind I heard an orchestra as I composed; Tim's playing almost made that real.

I began to close myself off from people once again. I had moved into a one-room bungalow with my piano and would only emerge to make tape recordings of the songs I was producing week after week. With each new song, I would disappear to Tim's place to play him a copy of my latest piece apologetically.

Tim had become my closest friend since Trish when I was seven years old. I began to sleep in Tim's room beside his bed.

My relationship with Tim was different from that with Bryn. I was not so afraid of my closeness with Tim; he had an ability to get close to me, but didn't capture me in the same way that Bryn had. With Tim, I was still able to escape into the characters when things got too much, yet when I was with him I felt it was okay to feel only three years old. I felt that at times he was only three years old, too.

Tim and I moved into a house together. From his room across the hallway, he would sing me to sleep. I let him brush my hair and invited him into my world.

Tim was the sort of person who accepted people exactly as he found them. Mentally Tim had his act together, though he was shy and, like me, hid behind a number of very convincing façades. Also like me, he had walked away from every person he had established seemingly close relationships with. Somehow I never became one of those statistics.

We established a marvelous sense of home. Everything in it was our special something or other. It was a three-year-old's paradise. In a childlike way, I grew to love Tim and he grew to love me. Sometimes we would talk so much that we would get no sleep.

We began to spend every waking moment together. It was the holidays, and we drove to work together, met for lunch, phoned each other up to say hello, and waited anxiously to see one another when we got home. The realization of how close we were becoming, as always, signaled the beginning of the end.

I began to fear Tim. There was a greater sort of depth in his eyes, and I became consciously aware that I had come to mean a great deal to him.

We went dancing together. I felt relatively safe in his company, as though he had the ability to scare off anything that frightened me. As we were dancing, sudden waves of fear washed over me. I looked into Tim's eyes, searching for a way out of the fear, which I could not express. Tim leaned over and told me that, if there was any woman he wanted to be with, I was that person.

It was like a slap in the face. I was frozen in time and space. My body continued to dance, but his words had killed off the sense of security I had found in him in one fell swoop. Tim became quite clearly an adult.

Carol stepped in as she had before: shallow, sociable, and skilled in the art of adult relationships. The house shook with laughter and music. Carol sang her heart out, and Donna disappeared. Carol looked up Stella's number in the phone book and invited around the girl who so long ago had used Carol's eccentric behavior as an excuse for her own. Stella loved to go out to nightclubs. Carol dragged Tim along.

IIII

"KAREN!" CRIED STELLA as she made her way across the room to the flamboyant woman in the leopard-print dress and fur coat. "You remember Karen, don't you?" said Stella. "Remember, I took you to meet her when we were kids?"

"Hi," said Carol, and sat down.

Karen went on and on about men. Her philosophy was simple: all men were woman-using pigs and it was up to women to get in and use them first. I told her that I had left the men in my life with everything, including many of my own things. She told me that it was about time I learned a thing or two about the facts of life.

Karen and Carol both loved gossip. The more this had to do with relationships, the more fired up became the conversation. The conversation turned to the topic of Tim. Karen insinuatingly asked about the situation with Tim, and Carol mirrored her expectations. Karen in her own perverse way decided to help misguided Carol devise a step-by-step plan to "capture" this man once and for all. Carol was not so aggressive and tried to back down, doubting whether Tim was interested in anything more than a platonic relationship and falling back on the excuse that she had already been through enough relationships and didn't want to "make the same mistakes." Karen interpreted this as lack of self-confidence and tried to help Carol to "send out the right messages."

||||

TIM WAS INTRIGUED by Carol's enthusiasm over her new-found friendship with Karen. He began to visit Karen himself. Karen had introduced the element of responsibility. Carol was supposed to take responsibility for helping Tim over his supposed shyness of relationships. This was a fatal mistake. Responsibility had never been Carol's realm.

The house began to rage with arguments, accusations, and long-winded analytical discussions. Willie, one of whose strongest points was responsibility, as always won the arguments.

Tim had decided to go and stay at a friend's place. He returned to the house with a friend to find me packing all of his things into boxes and placing them inside the door of his room.

"You're throwing me out," he accused.

"I'm not," I tried to reply, unable to get a word in edge-wise. I tried to explain that I simply couldn't bear to walk around the house with the feeling of Tim's things closing in on me, making me feel trapped with nowhere to run. I no longer felt safe in the presence of his things. I didn't want him to leave. I just didn't want to share my world with him anymore.

I wanted things back to the way they were long before, but the innocence of our relationship had been corrupted and he was now just another person. He moved out.

IIII

THE FINAL UNIVERSITY year came and went. I had passed with flying colors, and faced the uncertainty of what to do now that school had finished. I couldn't bear the thought. The university had been my only consistency throughout the chaos. It gave structure to my life while allowing me the distance of relating via books and theories. It had given me the independence of choosing what I wanted to learn and doing so in my own way at my own pace. It had also pro-vided me with a façade of normality. I decided to continue as an academic. For my thesis I chose the subject of "Devi-ance and Normality"; my material came from the lives of people, many of whom, as I once had, lived on the street.

What I had, as Willie, come to understand of my own evasive sense of belonging and self-expression became the basis for a theory that accounted for why some people use, abuse, or rip off themselves or others. It was part of my continuing effort to understand all of these aspects within my self, and I established, at the end, that the same mecha-nisms were at work in all people but that some were tied up in more knots, either mentally, emotionally, or socially, than others. It made me reflect on what Mary had done for me. She had helped me to untie the mental and the social knots, but the emotional ones were still haphazardly causing havoc.

For my thesis, I had chosen a supervisor whom I felt I

could relate to. In the end it was this very ability to relate that almost cost me the thesis.

I had basically chosen this professor for the sound of his voice. It was characteristic of a type of voice that I had found I could lose myself in. I didn't have to close him out, as he could go on and on without disturbing me. Also, his way of seeing the world did not appear to be too different from mine. He questioned the idea of any truly unquestionable reality, saw all things as relative, and like me had a working-class background that gave him some understanding of what it was like to sense a "them" and "us."

Throughout the course of writing this thesis, my behavior became more and more bizarre. I was extremely possessive of my work, refusing to show my supervisor any fragment of what I had been doing. I became extremely evasive when he asked me where my life fitted into my pursuit of this particular topic. He pursued an answer relentlessly, causing me to answer him with riddles. If I could have lied, it would have been easy, but any lie would have given away more about what I had to hide than my ability to hide and run away did.

My supervisor may have been sensitive but he was also sarcastic and at times cunning in trying to combat my evasiveness. He was, I believe, both surprised and amused by the way in which his sarcasm went over my head. Though I was clever in other ways, the subtlety of prompts and jibes was beyond my grasp. He eventually realized this and asked me in no uncertain terms why I was so evasive. He called me an enigma. I went home and looked it up in the dictionary.

He tried hard to reach me, but I was running as fast as I could. The often dangerous world in which I had immersed myself didn't help, and I sometimes wonder if I set myself up for turmoil and danger in an effort to shock myself into feeling something.

I think my supervisor wondered about this, too. He noticed the constant changes in my character, the most basic reflection of which was the way I dressed.

Like the characters I portrayed, my dress reflected my personality and its constant changes.

As a self who would rather have disappeared, I dressed uncharacteristically in hand-me-downs, which so appropriately expressed nothing of who I was. This was truest of me. On other days I would dress in a conservative, yet old-fashioned way, like a person old before her time, a self who had fought too many wars. Then, in striking contrast to this, I would dress loudly and provocatively. Like some walking piece of art, a mobile performance, I would strut into my supervisor's office, a self who had no feelings to be reached and no depth to be challenged.

My supervisor's caring concern did nothing for my thesis, though it did a lot for me. He was the one uninvolved mirror in my life at that time. The me his comments had captured stayed with me as snapshots in a photo album I looked through to remind myself of who and where I had been.

I had, for fear of him seeing it, avoided writing up the final draft of my thesis, or handing it in, waiting until the last possible moment. I had cut from it all richness of expression with the skill of a literary surgeon. There was not a personal element in it, except for a brief dedication. The animated extracts of information I had used to illuminate the text stood out as some perverse mockery of my own complete inability to expose myself emotionally to a waiting audience. The thesis was as clinical and sterile as a surgeon's instrument cabinet.

||||

TIM HAD BEGUN to come around to the house again, trying to salvage the friendship I had torn apart before his eyes. We fought furiously, him usually coming off second-best (though this was more indicative of the comparative strength of our fears than of anything else). We had begun to undo some of the damage when Karen moved in.

It was my birthday. Tim had been invited over to celebrate. Carol, Karen, and Tim stood around Karen's dining table, which was draped elegantly with an antique lace table-cloth. The wine was poured into the crystal glasses I had been given for my twenty-first birthday. The glasses were raised in a toast. "Happy birthday" came the announcement as the entire scene began to run in slow motion. Awake, yet in a dream state, Donna stood, frozen. My mouth hung open in shock. I had seen it all before, a few years ago, in a dream, exactly like this. Just when Carol had begun to think she was relatively normal, a realization came crashing down on her world. There was something very strange about the way this sort of thing continued to happen.

||||

THE UNIVERSITY YEAR finished. I was, at one stage, interested in continuing even further, but my fear of the exposing potential of long-term friendships was simply too great. My supervisor had, in my final week, begun to see me as I truly was.

I wondered if he realized that, as I handed him a goodbye gift: a riddlelike poem. I was terribly nervous. This was a huge effort at reaching out. The poem was a gesture to pay him back for his interest, patience, and support. Its contents was an attempt to explain the dilemma I was living and trying to overcome. He appreciated and was grateful for the gift. I truly wished he had accepted it with relative indifference. The acceptance of compliments or gratitude was something I had not yet quite mastered.

I was terribly afraid of what I was going to do next. I had done a lot of volunteer work in a variety of settings. This had given me some concrete social work experience within related fields that I could combine with everything I had studied, which would allow me to try for a "professional" job. I decided to try for social work positions. My many personal and professional references made for an impressive résumé. It wasn't long before I was offered two jobs. One was working with children, a lot of which I had already done. The other was working in a housing service for home-less people. I chose the latter.

IIII

DAVID WAS ONE of the hundreds of people I met in this new job, and he struck me as being the most unfortunate. He was the same age as me, yet was climbing as desperately toward self-ruin as I was trying to climb out of it. He appeared to symbolize who I had been at my most hopeless. Willie's protective instincts came to the fore, and Mary's role as psychiatrist was about to be put into practice. My office carried an open invitation for anyone who wanted to come in and discuss the hopes, the fears, and the dreams so many of them were drowning in alcohol daily. David called this office his second home, and Willie's sense of self-importance soared.

The staff at the center were disturbed by my approach, which they told me was all wrong. They were upset that I had achieved a higher profile among the clientele in two weeks than the previous social worker had achieved in two years. Furthermore, they insisted that I learn to socialize with the professionals and told me to spend my lunch hour up in the staff room. Willie had never had much respect for authority and quit the job after two weeks.

Meanwhile, David had sobered up in an effort to gain Willie's respect. It didn't work, but it boosted Willie's sense of self-importance and adequacy as some sort of social worker. David had heard I'd quit my job. I said goodbye and gave him my number in case he needed to talk sometime.

It wasn't long before he called, creating a drama that he'd been thrown out and needed a place to stay. Willie, who had spent a lot of time picking up other homeless representations of socially naïve Carols, came to the rescue and offered David a place to stay in the shack out in the back, so representative of the shacks and garages Carol had found shelter in years before.

David was a compulsive liar. In fact he was compulsive,

period. Immensely insecure, David used every piece of emotional blackmail in the book. Willie, who could run rings around others on an intellectual level, was completely lost when it came to tackling their emotional problems. Willie's detached and objective approach was being shot down in flames by this prize manipulator, who operated on a far more underhanded and emotional level. Carol, though without empathy, could appear to possess it. Her mental shallowness and social naïveté made her a prime target. She was about to be taken to hell and back.

IIII

WITHIN EACH OF us are the survival mechanisms of fight and flight. Willie was the personification of my response to fears outside myself—my fight response. Carol embodied my flight response: to run from fears that were sensed as coming from within—fear of emotion.

The new relationship that Tim and I had forged was again that of two innocent children. Tim tried hard to keep a grip on it, but at its most intense moments my fear of closeness came to the fore and Carol emerged ready to run.

Tim came around to see me. Unable to cope with the exposure of my feelings in front of anyone else, let alone an opportunist like David, I hid behind Carol, who tried to entertain and keep everyone laughing.

David found it all amusing. He watched as Tim brought me flowers at work. He listened as I spoke to Tim on the phone. He waited for a chance to shoot Tim down in flames.

"Do you know we're getting engaged?" David announced flippantly.

Tim's jaw dropped. His face hardened. There was tension in his voice as he said in a controlled manner: "Congratulations."

It was the first I'd heard of his proposal. I knew it was a game, but had I understood at that point its intentional cruelty or felt at ease with the depth of genuine feeling Tim had for me and I for him, I would have grabbed Tim by the hand

and run away from this monster who so cunningly disguised himself as an admirer.

Inside I was screaming. Inside I was reaching out to Tim. On the outside Carol held the stage, laughing and talking trivia, and ignoring the fact that David was cruelly rubbing Tim's face in the dirt. The scream and the tears and the desperation never registered in Carol's eyes. They were always shallow. They were always smiling. They were always dead.

||||

KAREN SAW DAVID for the worm that he was. She tried to warn me, saying she wanted him out. Willie, protecting him from being thrown out in the street, fought her accusations desperately. Stuck in time, Willie was protecting the mental image of Carol from a life on the streets; the same life that had led to her sellout as a domestic prostitute to men who didn't care that she was only a child.

Karen, in fury at my blindness, violently created dividing lines through the house, making it impossible for me to continue living there. She had condemned me to the very thing I was trying to avoid. I was once again homeless. David took me for everything I had managed to build up, including my sense of self.

David and I lived in the garage of a friend's house on a makeshift bed beneath greasy black wooden beams and spider webs. Carol settled into her role of domestic prostitute once again. As always, the eternal optimist in the face of adversity, she made light of the situation. David mocked her stupidity and dictated the plan of action. Carol followed blindly.

David didn't want to work. He was recovering. He wanted, however, to see the rest of the country, and the money from the sale of my things and my car were going to be his means of doing it.

David was quite at home in his position of torturer. He insisted that I do nothing without his permission. Even then he wanted to follow me. I couldn't go to the shop on my own. I couldn't talk to anybody unless he was there. I couldn't even go to the toilet on my own. He would wait for me outside the door and tell me off if I took too long. I was once again the poor, uneducated, battered wife.

Everybody David met despised him, which meant that I was unable to talk to anybody else even if I found the courage, as nobody could tolerate his company long enough to build up a friendship with me.

I began to think of Tim, and big silent tears would stream down my face.

"What's wrong with you?" David would demand.

"Nothing," I'd reply, painting a smile across my face. I needed to talk to Tim so desperately, and it was only thoughts of him that kept me going. Ironically it was fear of the closeness I felt for him that also kept me from going back.

llll

DAVID AND I had reached the other side of Australia. I was isolated, alone, and broke. It was the wet season in the tropics of the top end of Australia. I had become extremely weak, unable even to go walking for more than a few minutes at a time. I would begin to gasp for breath and feel faint. David had used my money for this joyride to visit his sister, and having run out of the money necessary to get my car to his destination he refused to work.

We were living in a dredge of a trailer park, but had to find cheaper accommodations. In the search from boardinghouse to boardinghouse, a woman had offered the possibility of a room in exchange for teaching her nephew English. David volunteered my services.

Teaching Carlos would be fairly straightforward, I thought. As it turned out, Carlos was ten years old and almost completely illiterate in both his native language, Greek, and in English.

I was very weak and had to spend the entire day in bed to

get enough energy to speak for the two-hour lesson with Carlos. I didn't know it at the time, but I was suffering severely from multiple food allergies and malnutrition, getting virtually no vitamins from anything I was eating.

Carlos was a delightful boy. I grew quite fond of him, and he and his sister grew quite fond of me. David was extremely jealous, but rent was rent. Carlos was coming along well, and even in my weakened state, he had aroused a sense of pride in me that conjured up the side of me I would need to get me out of this mess. I found the courage to write to Tim.

It was a stilted letter, with no return address. Nevertheless, my acknowledgment that I had had courage prompted me to take things one step further. I told David I was leaving. David, who'd had it pretty good so far, decided to come with me. I had to sell my car to cover the cost of both our tickets. I was returning to my own city.

IIII

WE TOOK A room in the backyard of a house. It was cramped and small, but I was back home in my own city. I telephoned Tim's mother and told her I was back. She asked if I wanted to see Tim. I told her I wasn't sure yet. She told me that Tim had been depressed since I'd left and that she was sure he'd be glad to know that I was back. I told her to tell him that I was doing fine and hung up.

After a few weeks I again rang Tim's mother. She had given him the message. She went on to tell me that he had just moved in with someone. She was upset about this as he'd already been through a lot and he hadn't known this person very long. I told her to give him my address.

Eventually Tim got in touch. We met in a takeaway shop —all four of us. It was awkward. Tim and his partner sat on one side, David and I on the other. We tried hard not to show how glad we were to see each other once again, but agreed to stay in touch.

I had begun to slap myself and pull out my own hair. I wanted desperately to get out of my own body, to leave it there to be stomped on, used, and abused as its invaders so chose. I was annoyed at this physical body and the way it held me in like the walls of an impenetrable prison. It seemed to me more than useless. I screamed, and my own ears were deafened, but no sound ever came out. I pleaded, but nothing got past the lips of my painted smile and the dead look in my eyes. I had a capacity for closeness, but my intense, relentless fear of it made closeness a sort of mocking, unreachable dream. This was the price of what may have been termed my autism. It went far deeper than the simplistic blanket description of "withdrawn."

I had managed to cry out to Tim for help, but Tim came with his partner. It seemed a cruel fate that she should have been so threatened by a child's closeness, for although I was an adult I was an adult trapped in a child's insecurity.

Tim responded like a policeman dealing with a domestic dispute. David had said I was completely mad. I had tried to explain what had happened. It was no use; everyone was a thousand miles away, and no sound came out.

I again took a job in a factory. The money I earned helped me to buy another trailer.

David had long since destroyed my friendship with Tim; and Tim, whose life in some ways was running parallel to mine, had begun to give up the battle to save it, convinced that he had obviously not meant as much to me as he had thought.

David and I moved into the trailer and again began to travel.

I began secretly to write to and phone Tim now that my transience made our closeness less threatening. Tim's letters were written as evasively as my own. They held messages about holding on to oneself and not blaming oneself for the compulsive need to run away. I knew those letters by heart. In the end it was the strength these had given me, and the hope that despite my compulsion to behave in contradiction to all I was there was still one person who had never given up on me, and had almost always continued to fight to see me for who I truly was, that helped me to reach a decision.

One evening, in the dead of night, I put a plan into action. I was leaving David.

I ran away, into the night, in another strange city, surrounded by strangers. I had spoken to a stranger on a telephone advice service who had fortunately challenged my ability to have the guts to leave. This was exactly what I needed in order to fight back and have something to prove.

I sneaked back to the trailer and silently slid a note through the door. The note instructed David to meet me at a particular place in the city at a particular time the next day. I sneaked away back to the car I had parked, lights out, motor running. I drove to the other side of this strange city, parked the car, and fell asleep, cold, hungry, and homeless.

The next day I returned to the trailer at the time I had told David to meet me elsewhere. I took all of my personal belongings and left everything else, including the trailer and my piano, for him to keep so he would never bother me again. I had wasted a year and half of my life with this beast. Whatever I lost, it was worth it.

I drove through the night until I saw double. I was extremely tired and hungry and had only enough money to get back to my own state, if that. I slept in the car, in a carpark, parked next to a trailer full of barking dogs. I was the happiest I had been since I had lived with Tim in the early days. For once, this was a real happiness. I felt it inside and, for a change, it was reflected by the expression on my face, which was peaceful.

||||

I ARRIVED AT Tim's place by surprise. Tim's partner was understanding about my predicament, aware of everything I had gone through and the strength of the friendship between Tim and me. I stayed long enough to get a job and a place to live, then left as quietly as I had come.

I moved into a shared house in a beautiful semirural area far across the other side of town from Tim. The owner of the house had a little girl who was two. The little girl responded to me, and I began to open up and come out of my shell. I began to go out on my own. I had never done this as my real self and, unlike Carol, I had no intention of being social.

||||

A GROUP OF young men sat across from me and began to try to talk to me. They were Irish, and I couldn't understand a word they were saying, and when they persisted I told them so. One of them looked into my eyes intently. He was silent and signaled in the direction of the dance floor with his eyes. I silently responded.

We went to his friend's place. It seemed quite acceptable to me to be in their company and yet refuse to socialize. My answers were short and invited no conversation as I examined my surroundings. His friends gave up trying to speak to me. The man hardly spoke and appeared at ease and intrigued by my silence and detachment, so there was no real threat.

Neither of us wanted to be in a relationship. Our desire simply to be in each other's company suited both of us just fine. We knew we did not want to feel attachment or any sort of mental familiarity with one another. This was the beginning of the most equal, undemanding, and unstressful relationship I had so far ever had. In silence and unfamiliarity, it was also the only way in which I could feel unthreatened while indulging in what pleasure there was to be gained from being touched.

This man was dyslexic and had communication problems similar to mine. Our past was simply irrelevant. Most of it would have been in contradiction to my real self in any case. We kept all conversation to a minimum and communicated largely through sense. Our overwhelming sensitivity meant that the relationship was far more sensual than sexual. We saw one another for three months. In his own way, he began to try to get to know me. We began to lose touch.

||||

I AGAIN BEGAN to become very ill. The asthma and muscular pains I'd suffered from when I was with David were back. I began to fall asleep in the middle of the day and nothing seemed able to wake me. Other times I would find that I had been staring into space doing nothing for hours at a time.

My ability to concentrate on anything was very poor. I would watch the television with no conception of what I was seeing but for a series of colors, patterns, and movement. The only thing that seemed able to snap me out of this was the television commercials, whose simplistic tunes and jingles would stick in my mind, replaying for hours, days, or even weeks on end.

One day I left a building through the same door I had come in, yet I found that somehow the building had changed places. It was not on the same side of the street as before. I walked back into the building, turning my back on the street outside, then I walked back out again. It was still opposite from the way it had been when I had originally gone in.

I was afraid. I asked what the name of the street was. It was the same street. I had parked my car further down the street, but now, with no sense of direction whatsoever, I had no idea where it might be.

"Please, which way is Mitchell Street?" I asked, though I had grown up in this city and knew the streets like the back of my hand.

"Over there," said the voice, pointing.

I followed the direction of the arm and became alarmed. How on earth did Mitchell Street get down there?

I began to cry; I was afraid. A stranger's voice asked me what was wrong.

"I'm lost," I explained. "I have no idea how to find my car."

"What sort of car is it?" said the voice. I explained, saying that I had parked it in the same street I was standing in but could not say in which direction. The man who was helping me spotted it. I ran to my car.

The whole world seemed to have turned itself upside

down, inside out, and back to front. Everything was like a mirror image of what it had been when I had entered the building.

I climbed into my car and sat there frightened. I knew the names of the streets and had never had any trouble finding my way around. But now just like driving into a mirror image, I found myself, street after street, at the wrong end, opposite the direction I wanted to go. I ended up on the wrong side of town completely. Instead of driving toward home, I had, as in a mirror, driven away from it.

This happened on and off for two days. I became terribly afraid that I had gone mad. I realized that, whether I was mad or not, I needed a job where I was standing in one place all day.

||||

I APPROACHED A theatrical shop. I had fallen in love with the wall of feather, velvet, and sequin masks, the wigs of every length and style, and the huge life-size bear costume that was suspended from the ceiling by string and stood by the counter threatening customers. I could relate to that.

The owner wanted someone with five years' retail experience. Carol sold her on the value of an outgoing personality and a terrific ability to communicate the desirability of the intriguing bits and bobs around the store. It was decided that Carol's sheer enthusiasm for the products the shop offered would help sell the things if anything would.

Carol dressed up in rabbit ears and furry costumes day in and day out. Out of curiosity children would drag their parents into the store, and often the parents would be conned into buying something I was wearing. One day I even got into the very expensive bear suit and went dancing about in the street. A man came in and bought it to take back to the bush town he was from to surprise his friends and entertain his children.

The shop's sales doubled, despite the fact that I had to be told continually to pay more attention to the customers than to the compulsive rearrangement of the merchandise. One little girl, captured by the charm of my evasiveness, came up to me and tapped my arm.

"Are you a real fairy?" she asked.

"Yes," I said.

"Can I touch you to see if you are real?" she added.

"I'm sorry," I said. "I may disappear if you touch me."

There is no doubt a place for everyone, I suppose.

The entire roof of this shop was a mass of fluorescent lights. I was becoming terribly ill, finding it hard at times even to find the energy to lift an arm. I began to wear a sun visor, and this prevented me from falling asleep under the effect of the dazzling lights.

My boss thought I was completely mad, but I suited the nature of the shop and my eccentricity seemed to attract customers.

I began to get rheumatic pains again, and my muscles were so tense that I tore a muscle in my arm simply by reaching out for something. I began to turn bluish, tremble, and then faint. I had dark circles under my eyes. I began to take vitamins, but they did not seem to help.

I had the same symptoms I'd had as a child; my gums bled, and I bruised at the slightest touch. In desperation I once again went looking to find a vitamin that might patch me up.

IIII

I CONSULTED A naturopath, a physician who treats patients solely by modifying their diet. Instead of selling me any more vitamins, she asked if there was any particular type of food I ate all the time. This sounded like a strange question, and she explained to me that my symptoms may have been due to a lack of vitamins but that this deficiency may have been a problem of absorption. She explained that it was pos- sible that I was suffering from intolerance to various food substances and that some of these may have been in the vitamin tablets themselves. Additionally she explained that

I may have been using up what little vitamins I was absorbing in trying to rid my body of the buildup of toxins due to undigested foods. I explained to her how I would partially recover soon after getting away from the fluorescent lights I worked under. She explained that allergic reactions can have several components and that the effect of the lights may have been the straw that broke the camel's back. She gave me a card with a number on it. It was the phone number of an allergy clinic specializing in food intolerance.

In the meantime, I went off some of the foods I was eating so compulsively. After dropping potatoes and tomatoes, my rheumatism and muscular trouble went away for the first time in months. I dropped dairy foods, and the dark circles under my eyes and my asthma disappeared. I cut down on my high refined-sugar intake, and the fainting and tremors faded almost completely away. At the same time I began to binge on a whole range of other foods, and by the time of my appointment with the allergy clinic, I had developed problems with some of these foods, too.

I eventually went to two clinics. Both of the clinics were established and run by medical practitioners who had undertaken their own private research into the effects of diet on health.

The first of these clinics operated along the lines of Western medicine, the second along the lines of Eastern medicine. As very few doctors were well read on the subject of food intolerance, the appointments were very expensive and only partially covered by government funds.

I had previously spent the last few years on and off asthma medication—me going off it, and the doctors telling me I was foolish and putting me back on it.

In previous years the so-called hospital specialists had given me "scratch tests," whereby drops of a substance are placed on the skin in order to see if the skin reacts allergically. On the basis of these tests I was dismissed as not suffering from allergies. However, I had only been tested for airborne allergens.

Intolerance to different foods can cause allergic reactions

in different parts of the body. In my case my skin was not the "target organ" for my particular allergic reactions. It was not until the clinic used the method of injecting me with various food substances that it was discovered that I was indeed suffering from extreme multiple food allergies.

At the first clinic, using a series of blind tests, they found that I was allergic to all meat except beef, all dairy products, eggs, soy products, potatoes, tomatoes, and corn. I was also put through a six-hour blood-sugar test and found to be suffering from severe hypoglycemia.

What this effectively meant was that I had to eat every two hours in order to avoid a sudden and dramatic drop in my blood-sugar level. Any degree of excitement only exacerbated this, causing me to tremble, turn blue, and faint as my nervous system responded to a sudden, dangerous plummet in my blood-sugar level. Every step on the way down was a step-by-step change in my conscious awareness of my surroundings. Furthermore, in response to this condition, my body was releasing its own adrenaline, causing me to speed up, which I usually channeled into the character of Carol.

I had previously lived on an extremely high-sugar diet. I was now required to maintain a diabetic diet. After three days off sugar, I had extreme and violent withdrawal reactions.

Though I had rid myself of chronic rheumatism and asthma, there was still something triggering changes in my behavior. I heard of the other clinic and decided to try it.

This clinic used a method of testing that operated along some of the principles of acupuncture. They used electronic equipment to test the effects of food chemicals upon the body's electromagnetic field. I was found to be allergic to a group of chemicals called phenolics and salicylates, which are common to many fruits, vegetables, herbs, and spices, and almost all prepackaged foods. In particular, my extreme intolerance of phenolics was found to be twice as great as that usually considered to be a high reading.

Although many of those foods contain substances beneficial to most people, those same substances were slowly poisoning me and robbing my body of vitamins. At this clinic I was tested both for the vitamins I was lacking and for my ability to tolerate them, regardless of the beneficial properties they may have had for others who were not so allergically sensitized.

Sticking to this diet was nearly impossible, but work had also become impossible owing to my ill health, and I was worried about the threat of homelessness, should I get sick.

I stayed on the diet for a year, avoiding most foods that I knew to contain the proteins and properties to which I was allergic. This meant that my diet consisted almost entirely of homemade foods, mostly grains.

After the first few weeks, my boss at the costume shop was amazed. I had begun to talk calmly and patiently to the customers, even when they became impatient with me. My mood swings had become less pronounced, and my ability to get along with people improved, too. I became far more peaceful and shy than boisterous, manic, and aggressive. Still, though this resolved my physical ill health and made me a lot more stable, my deep-rooted emotional insecurity and the social communication problems that arose from it still remained.

||||

I HAD BECOME a far quieter person. I was afraid of what seemed like a new me. It was as though I had stepped into a new pair of shoes with an eerie old feeling about them. I had not yet fully acknowledged that Donna was finally on her way out into "the world." I wanted desperately to escape back into my characters. I needed to destroy all the security I had built up in order to create enough stress to bring on the anxiety that had always been the boundless energy behind my characters. A friend of mine was going to England. Whoever I was, I decided I was going to England, too. I packed my things and told Tim and Mary, my old psychiatrist, that I was leaving the country.

Though Mary had invited me to her house, I had never

invited her to mine. I decided that, in spite of my fear, I was finally going to invite her to my place.

Mary arrived, and I darted around the room like a nervous puppy. I hardly sat in one place all night. Nevertheless, I had known Mary for nine years by this stage, and it was a major achievement for me to have found the courage to allow her into this now depersonalized flat to view a snapshot of my private life. At the time, I still found it near impossible to be myself. My characters had always been so much more impressive than I.

Saying goodbye to Tim was another matter. Tim had long since left the partner he was living with. He was as close to me as he had ever been. He knew that in calling him up after not having seen him for some time I was again, in my own way, showing him that I felt something for him. The problem was that, as myself I felt too much for everything and therefore had to run away. Had I not had the escape of being led off to England, I would not, under such emotional circumstances, have been able to face seeing Tim. I always had to have a door to run out of.

I told both Tim and Mary that I wanted no one to come and see me off at the airport and told Tim that he was not to come to my house with any last goodbyes.

Tim ignored me. He was the only person who knew that Donna didn't really want to go. Yet Tim was in many ways like me; he knew I was compelled to go.

Tim arrived on the day I was to leave. He arrived at the flat with a prepared breakfast and a vulnerable look in his eyes. I felt exposed and trapped. Willie snapped at him. Tim didn't care; this was too important.

I so admired Tim's courage as he tried hard to ignore Willie's hateful and cutting remarks. He was told he wasn't wanted and asked to go. Tim took my hand and kissed me gently. He was pushed away. Tim stood watching me at war within myself, all because I couldn't stand the pain of feeling closeness. He left. I left for England.

||||

I LOOKED THROUGH the many bags and tins of little treasures that I had packed in a tea-chest for the trip. I piled in the bits of colored tinfoil, buttons, ribbons, sequins, and colored glass that had been with me all my life.

In the end the tea-chest lid wouldn't go down, and I sorted through all of my bits several times before weeding out the ones I was least taken by or attached to. I folded and packed all the lesser-loved bits neatly into a carrier bag and thought of who I could give them to.

The places, experiences, and people I had become attached to, my sense of security, and my ability to make sense of the relationships between things existed within these collections. I could lay everything out in categories and grasp the concept of order, consistency, and belonging despite my inner lack of it. I could see what role each thing had in relation to the next, unlike my relationships with people. Unlike my life, all my special things had their own undeniable place within the scheme of things.

No matter how much people told me that I fitted in or was accepted, I couldn't feel it. I once wrote: "Words on the wind, when they're calling you in, the words, have no meaning when the thoughts have no feelings." When I set out my bits and pieces, I could visually grasp the elusive sense of belonging I could never feel with people, and through this could give myself hope that it would one day be possible. I could see it, laid out in front of me in categories of things that could be arranged slowly and gently to blend into one another in some concrete, observable, and totally orderly way.

||||

I HAD JUST had my twenty-sixth birthday. It was the usual inner loneliness in an even lonelier place. After three months in England, during which I'd supported myself by temping, my precious bits arrived. I spent some time looking through them before closing the lid on them once more. I did not put any around the room, I did not show them off or try to explain their individual meaning—my language. I lived far more in my things than I did in my body. Leaving them packed away, uncorrupted, meant that they were retrievable later when it would be safe yet again to get close to myself and my feelings.

My mental state was such that any degree of fear over what I was to say made it impossible to express myself directly. The mental tricks I would play on myself in order to communicate condemned me to be judged by them. I was convincing my audience that I was the complete antithesis of what I truly was. What they saw as shallow, I experienced as deep. What they saw as clever, I found simple to reel off without any personal significance. While people around me judged me by their eyes and ears, I was screaming out from beneath the empty façade of my shell to get them to feel who I was; to close their eyes and their ears, and to try to sense me.

I found that people were usually blinded by their own insecurities or egotism or selfishness. They seemed so ignorant in their self-assured black-and-white conception of "normality." Every so often, however, one of them would wonder whether others had something to learn from me in trying to understand my differentness. Some people, like Mary and Tim, could sense the courage it took to teach myself so many things, to write the music I wrote with such depth and passion.

||||

I HAD SEEN an advertisement to perform comedy. I had already dabbled in this, writing comical mockeries of the world around me. I met the manager, who was running the courses in the hope of discovering new performers. He found me somehow naturally funny when I was least trying to be. We worked together to script some of these things, and he offered me the course free if I'd do short fill-ins for his paid comedians.

Comedy was a means of getting people to experience my

world. It made them laugh where they might otherwise cry. Comedy is most truly about alienation. Both Carol and Willie —my defense mechanisms embodied—were right at home with alienation. The fear of self-exposure was a mechanism by which I could shock myself. This fear came mostly from within. Armed only with a smile and a comedy script based on my childhood, Carol took the stage.

The laughs came relatively easily. Here was a woman, in the image of a girl, naïvely and casually relaying a series of horrific and tragic events from my life, without any element of emotion for the person who had fallen victim to them, because Carol had no self. The situation spelled out my reality cruelly and blatantly. I was unable to feel most of the things that had happened to me and of which I had seemed to be a part. The audience was, for a change, as alienated as I was.

They could not believe that what I was saying, and how I was saying it, was anything other than a joke, yet every bit of it was closely aligned to reality. I was trying to show them the hypocrisy of a life without feeling while confirming my own lack of hope that, even if pushed to the limits, I might discover some feeling for my life that I had not felt before.

Quite simply, it came down to the fact that I had never experienced "the world" with the walls down. The distinction between Carol standing alone on the stage and the collective, social, and communal atmosphere of the laughing audience down there summed it up in all its poetic tragedy: "my world" versus "theirs."

I had not done too badly. One of the acts had his own venue and asked if I'd like to do a paid spot as a support act. I had managed to fall into my first paid comedy performance.

The reality of it all became a slap in the face. The whole effort had been an act of self-expression, a scream at the hypocrisy of my situation. The idea of doing comedy as a skill for which I was to be paid simply cheapened it all the more. I phoned up the manager of the show and impersonally left a message on his answering machine telling him that on the spur of the moment I had gone to Europe.

||||

THERE WAS ABSOLUTELY no reason to go to Europe except that I hadn't yet been there. My job as a temporary secretary had just ended, and with no familiar surroundings I couldn't imagine being any more lost than I already was. Before leaving for Europe, I decided, out of the blue, to go and be by the ocean. I ran out of my room, grabbing only my toothbrush, and made my way to the train station.

I had always been plagued by a terrifying repetitive dream of the ocean. Without realizing its significance, something quite unconscious was driving me to confront this symbolic representation of my dilemma.

"Where's a good place to go, where there is ocean?" I demanded from the girl behind the counter.

"You want me to choose?" she asked, surprised.

"Yes, pick a place," I ordered.

She picked a place in South Wales and I paid for the ticket.

"Where are you going to?" asked a pleasant old lady sitting next to me on the platform.

"Don't know. Can't pronounce it. It's Welsh," I explained.

I was disturbed at not being able to pronounce my destination and turned to a stranger sitting beside me, at the top end of the platform. The stranger pronounced it, and I tried to memorize it. The train came along, and we all got on. I liked to sit near to the door. The stranger had by chance decided to sit by the door, too. He sat opposite me, and we both looked out of the window.

There was something about this man's manner. He was making me terribly nervous by his obvious shyness and embarrassment at sitting opposite me. I could relate to his behavior too well. I had recognized it as my own language and began to feel nervous and exposed at someone else being privy to it.

The Welsh stranger made a series of statements, in a manner addressed more to himself than to me. I was alarmed yet intrigued, embarrassed by how exposing and vulnerable it felt to be communicated with in my own manner. Not since my friendship with Bryn so many years before had I found someone who spoke the evasive language of indirectness so well.

The train journey took three hours. Both of us sat there, nervous, exposed, and embarrassed. Though intrigued, we both sat poised to run at the first opportunity. To have done so of our own volition, however, would have been too exposing, in that it would have indicated choice. To one who spoke the language, this would have demonstrated the frightening nature and realness of the contact we had made. We sat there, swapping trivia, talking via objects and events, and losing our self-awareness in the evasive jargon and complexity of the poetrylike speech that so often got our listeners lost.

Surprisingly we had understood each other. There was a recognition of our shared differentness. We were both curious.

The Welshman was to get off one stop before my destination. He couldn't ask, and I knew how that felt.

"You can get off here if you want," he stated. I admired him, for in saying that he had had more courage than I would have been able to find. I sat there, shocked in the wake of finding someone who understood my ways because they were his own. "I'll flip a coin," he said. He flipped it and lost the toss. "I've got another one," he stated, with a hint of desperation. He flipped it, and it dropped to the floor and rolled away as the train pulled into the station.

He stood at the doorway looking at me. His eyes and smile, forced in their casualness, defied the stifled expression of a want that he was too trapped to express. "You can still get off here," he stated, unable to ask. Though afraid, I made a last-minute decision and jumped off the train as it ground to a halt.

||||

"YOU'RE CRAZY," HE had said, his excitement calling for a need to create distance. He had hit upon a sore point by saying that.

"Thanks," I said bluntly.

"It's great, though," he added in a hurried awkwardness.

We were both shaking, surprised at our own gameness.

We went to a café. He sat across the table. His foot touched mine accidentally, and I was painfully aware of it. Yet at the same time, as it was frightening, I was too afraid to move away as this would have shown that it mattered. I let my expression ignore it. I trembled; my feelings were screaming for me to run for my life.

He offered to pay for what I'd eaten. I insisted on paying. It bought me out of any obligation and got around the problem of being unable to accept generosity. It didn't work. He worked by the same system. He insisted that he then had to buy me a drink later on that night. A time and a place were arranged.

I found myself a room in a bed-and-breakfast and, terrified, went to my room, glad to be alone. I contemplated escaping, not because I felt nothing for this man but because I sensed that he knew my way of functioning too well. He could get close to me. Nevertheless, when I had agreed to something, I always had to stick to it. I went to the hotel to meet him.

I waited, petrified. I bought myself two glasses of wine in order to calm down. I hated the fact that there were people around me. Other people had no part in this. What I felt was simply too personal to allow other people even to glance at me. Hopeful, I asked whether the hotel had a piano.

The piano sat alone in a huge and glorious dining room. I sat at the keyboard, hoping I would first hear the stranger coming, and hesitantly began to play.

The stranger entered the dining room. Acutely aware of how personal it was to me, I tried convincingly to say that I was no longer interested in playing.

"Go on," he said. Obediently I began to play, losing my place and playing stiltedly as I lost the ability through concentrating too hard. The stranger was moved by my music. We were both shaking and nervous at feeling so real. I suggested we leave.

The freedom of walking made it safer to talk. Walking was, after all, one step away from running. It was that open door I always needed to feel safe.

We walked for hours in the darkness. We walked to the ocean, and in my mind I sang a song to the sea. I looked desperately at the stranger and wished that, for once, I had the courage to share this with another person. Even thinking this was terrifying. Walking back up the shore, I found the courage to sing out loud, to myself, unable to let even my own mind know that my singing was a means of communication.

This stranger understood my language. He spoke it himself. He never invaded. He never complimented. He never made it obvious that he was sharing. He simply stayed within my company, "being."

I felt so "found," I could have cried. As always, the tears could never make it to my eyes. I laughed, and my fear hid behind a casual façade.

We went walking in the darkness toward the rolling hills. We climbed on someone's farm equipment—two three-year-olds in a playground all their own. He reached out to give me a hand to climb up. My heart sank. I became painfully aware of my inability to combine touch and feeling.

We'd turned back toward the town. Walking alongside him, I felt a strange sensation. The hair stood up on the back of my arms, and we stared at each other in shock.

Like the little girl in the theatrical shop had done a year before, he reached out hesitantly and touched the back of my arm.

"Are you real?" he asked.

Stunned, I managed to say, "Yes."

"It felt like you just walked through me," he said.

"I know," I said, my mind lost in some strange hypnotic state. "I felt it, too."

It was as though the wind had blown straight through me.

My eyes scanned my hands and feet, surprised that I did, in fact, have a physical body.

I had always experienced being touched emotionally as the threat of death. The tremors associated with this were equivalent to being in a near-death situation where the only thing your mind is saying is "Get me out of here; I'm going to die." I had finally confronted this fear of death that washed over me like ocean waves. I had heard the roaring sound of silence in my ears and lost all sense of self-awareness as I stayed with the deathlike fear emotion gave me. I had found myself in a state of shock through allowing myself to keep a grip on feeling. Yet I had survived. No characters emerged automatically to take over. Donna was beginning to win the battle. This time, however, she was not fighting to mirror someone else. She was fighting to come out to someone who was *her* mirror.

We sat talking more to ourselves than to each other, allowing the other to listen in, until the sun began to come up. I felt I had known this man my entire life.

All words were irrelevant. I sensed this stranger's familiarity as though it were myself sitting next to me. I had failed to respond to the fear that seemed to feed on my closeness like a vulture. In failing, I had won.

We stood silently watching the waves crashing. It was noon the next day, and my train was due in an hour. I'd come further in the one day I'd known this stranger than I had in years of meeting those who had no hope of reflecting me enough to reach me as only I could reach myself. There was no hug goodbye. Not even a handshake. Even to look at each other was overwhelming and exposing. Yet, knowing my fear, knowing his, and knowing the need to try to learn to ignore it, we made an unbreakable promise to stay in touch, then I turned without saying goodbye and ran the length of the street, around the corner and to the station for the train to take me back to my things in London.

||||

A LETTER ARRIVED. The stranger's words echoed my own feelings and experiences. I couldn't believe they were real and that he was every bit the reflection of me I'd perceived him to be. I had to see him once again before I disappeared to Europe.

I arrived unexpectedly at the address he had given me. His family were warm and welcoming and didn't seem the least bit alarmed by the surprise of my visit.

He was in his room. I entered and stood in the doorway. I was shaking like a leaf, and so was he. Wanting a way out, wanting to be made to run, so that I had the choice made for me, I asked if I had made a mistake in coming. He explained that, had he known I was coming, he would have gone out, not knowing how to cope. He said I could stay. I was desperately fighting the impulse to run, feeling like I was drowning in the depth and intensity of having feelings, but I stayed nevertheless.

Everything was the same as before. Nothing had changed. My intense fear was making me talk at a hundred miles an hour. Surprisingly he kissed me for the first time. I broke into tears. He asked what I was crying about, and I covered my tracks. Yet I had been crying because it was the first time in my life I had really "been there" while I had been kissed.

His parents were ecstatic. They'd never seen their son talk so much or be so sociable with a friend. During the day we watched TV, played music, and hardly emerged from the insular security of his room. During the night we went walking through the darkness of the Welsh countryside so representative of our own darkness, so rarely lit by the presence of another person who walked within "our world" and "the world" at the same time.

After two days we caught the train together that would see us go our separate ways. He had to go away for three months. I had already decided to go to Europe.

I firmly nailed down the lid of my tea-chest of belongings and left wondering if I'd return with enough courage to see the Welsh stranger again.

I was wide-eyed and felt terribly vulnerable as I faced the prospect of traveling alone throughout Europe. I was afraid of being cornered by people I might meet, of their talking rings around me and manipulating me into situations I couldn't get out of. The stranger had offered me the opportunity to stay with his parents until he returned. Frightened, I had desperately wanted to hide in his room full of security. Yet the inability to reach out or accept anything still crippled me, making his offer impossible to accept.

||||

I HAD ALWAYS wanted to see Holland, and imagined myself skating alone on fields of endless white ice. But I'd missed the ferry to Holland, and the next one was going to Belgium. I didn't even know there was a country called Belgium, but at the risk of sleeping at the ferry terminal I caught the last ferry to Belgium arriving before midnight.

The stranger had given me an empty bottle that he had filled with invisible hugs, just in case, in the privacy of my solitude, I might like to give them to myself. The vulnerability of remaining feeling while surrounded by the world of strangers into which I had thrown myself was too much of a threat. I got a room at eleven fifty-five P.M. Alone in my hostel room on my first night abroad in greater Europe, I opened the bottle and allowed myself to feel the security I had felt when the stranger and I had locked ourselves away in his room. I put my arms around myself and rocked as tears ran silently down my face. I screamed deafeningly within my mind. The bottle of hugs seemed to mock my inadequacy. I wanted no one to see it. I hid it in the darkness of a corner in the back of an obscure cupboard. That empty bottle stood for myself. I would travel alone without any emotions to haunt me.

||||

I AWOKE AND went out into the misty morning along the cobblestoned streets of Ostend. Ducks on chilly ponds, a horse and cart, shop windows filled with handmade lace butterflies and old-fashioned collars. I walked across a narrow town bridge and laughed at how the buildings along the canal reached right down into the water. Where on earth were the buildings' legs? I wondered. What is the way of life here, what language do these people speak, and what country is Belgium next to?

I went to what appeared to be a small shop and looked for the door. There was only a window and a lot of very unusual-looking food. I was addressed in a language I couldn't understand, and it struck me that I couldn't even ask this shopkeeper where the door was so that I could go in and buy something. Then it dawned on me that, for some strange reason, these shops in this strange place had no doors for the customers to go in. One was supposed to order from the window. I looked at the food and wondered what the hell was in it and whether, with my allergies, it would make me sick. I reckoned that not eating was just as likely to make me sick, so in response to the shopkeeper's gabble I pointed at something and offered him a handful of change I'd got at the ferry terminal.

Not knowing where to go, I walked toward the station. Trains took people places. Travel was a universal language. One didn't need to speak; one had only to go. I would go to find the ice in Holland.

I listened to the voices around me and caught the train to the name of a place that sounded familiar: Amsterdam.

I arrived in Amsterdam as it was getting dark. Scruffy people kept shoving pamphlets into my hands about hostels to stay in. I stopped and bought a hot dog at a stall, and a photographer approached me and began to take photos. I glared at him from beneath my black hat. In my high-collared black coat, black hat, and rucksack, I looked like a Quaker. I hadn't understood the photographer's interest till he turned his camera on some nearby children. What was it he saw? Perhaps innocence.

I was pointed in the direction of a Christian hostel and given some good advice on where not to stay and walk about alone at night in Amsterdam.

At the door of my hostel room I froze at the realization that I would be in a room with about twenty other women.

The next day I went out to look for a job. For some reason it never occurred to me that the rules for any country would be any different from those in England. It was simple, I thought. I'd get some temporary work as a secretary or a cleaner. I was very wrong. I arrived back at the hostel feeling depressed and disillusioned. There was no work for an Australian in Amsterdam—at least, not what *I* considered work. I had only enough to pay for my dinner. It was time to find a cash machine and get some money. Was I in for a shock!

I asked where I could use my card, and my heart sank and I felt sick at the reply. There was nowhere in the Netherlands, let alone in Amsterdam. The nearest branch for my account was in Paris. Even with a visa it would have cost me more than I had to get there. I used the last of my money to call my bank in England, and somewhere between tears, swearing, and mutual misunderstanding my money ran out on the phone call and left me totally penniless in a foreign country.

I went back to the hostel hysterical. The staff managed to calm me down and said they'd help. My room would be free, and I would work in the kitchen in exchange for meals until my money came through from England. They gave me the money to call again. This time I got through.

I was told that protocol was protocol and I would have to send them signed permission to transfer funds to Amsterdam. It would take several days, and there was a limit to the amount I could receive.

In the meantime a roommate from the hostel asked if I'd go sight-seeing around the city with her. After all, it might cheer me up. We were hungry, and I was sick of people supporting me. I took off my hat, laid it on the footpath in the main street, and began to sing. The money fell like rain from heaven. It wasn't much, but it was enough to buy some bread and a cup of tea.

A slick, fairly streetwise type approached us and gave us some advice. He picked up my hat and shoved it into my friend's hands. "This is how you do it," he said, and instructed her to walk directly up to the passersby with my hat as I sang. He had been busking for about three years and was only too willing to tell us how to be successful. I sang a bit more, and then we all went for coffee.

Before my money arrived from England I sang for a few hours every day and learned the best busking places around Amsterdam's city square. I bought my roommate and myself bread and tea every day, paid for my hostel room, and even bought something I'd always wanted: a tambourine.

My money came through, and my roommate had a wonderful idea of what to do with it. She asked me to go to Germany with her. We boarded the train for Berlin where she knew some friend of a friend of a friend.

This woman was surprised to meet her, and even more surprised to meet me, but she was a medical student and a really nice person and glad to have the two of us suddenly drop in on her. My traveling companion was keen to show off the singing and tambourine-playing talents of her weird friend, and I was glad to latch on to her apparent sense of destination. Together we made our way around Berlin as I sang and bought them bread and tea. At the Berlin Wall I got some sense of perspective. I had heard of it on the news and was glad to be with something familiar. We went into East Berlin at the time when the Wall was still protected by armed guards as those from the West chipped away at it with rented hammers and sold pieces of graffiti-covered stone from it.

One night the others went out, leaving me alone in the German woman's flat, listening to Chris de Burgh singing "Borderline." My roommate from Amsterdam met two German travelers willing to give us a ride to Austria. She returned and told me the news. By now I was almost broke yet again, and it was a relief to know we had a cheap means of transport. Together we met the women the next day and headed south. At Freiburg my roommate decided to travel with one of the women to her home in the Black Forest. The other woman was going to a fairy-tale village in the province of Hesse. The sound of a castle overlooking a town full of twisting cobblestoned streets seemed like something I'd dreamed up.

IIII

I FELL IN love with the place instantly. All the streets were narrow and cobblestoned, with little staircases cropping up to take you down to the next street below. There were hills that seemed to roll on forever. I let my mind fly over them. I could see open space for miles.

I had not been able to find a place to stay. I started to hitchhike and was picked up by a young German man. I spoke no German and, thinking he spoke no English, felt fairly safe. As it turned out, his English was fine. He was a residential worker in a children's home and was on his way to stay there for the next two nights. He offered me a room at the home. I was momentarily stunned at destiny having presented me with the opportunity to stay in that horror of all horrors, a children's home. Nevertheless, having nowhere else to go, I accepted.

Julian was an intense though gentle person. Like me, he wrote poetry and music within which, like me, he was most truly himself.

As always, the children took to me wonderfully. They led me about telling me the names of things in German, which, to their delight, I would repeat, listening to the sound.

Julian watched me secretly as I watched the children. He began to study me. "Stop looking at me," I snarled, as I so often did when people tried to study me. Julian smiled knowingly. He seemed no stranger to my behavior, perhaps having seen it in another person somewhere. He said nothing and went on observing, at times when I least expected.

He played music and asked me to sing, never waiting for a response as to whether I would or not. He had used the right tactics, as he continued to play, seeming really not to care whether I joined in or not. I began to sing. "That's great," he said, his head still bowed as he played guitar. He had invited a friend over to hear me sing.

As though now more self-assured with his friend there, he all of a sudden looked straight into my eyes. My heart sank with fear as I sat there, abandoned by my characters.

As though my frightened look had confirmed his own preconceptions, he reached forward and brushed my cheek with the back of his hand, as though taming a delicate and frightened little bird. I glared at him in terror and moved away. He was tiptoeing through a mine field and was taking everything a step at a time. I was an easy victim. Fortunately, he had no intention of treating me like one.

Julian was intrigued by why I was so totally different at different times, though, unlike most people, he was perceptive enough to notice that these changes were fear responses rather than true expressions of my personality. After spending several days with me and only being able to get close to Carol, he looked deeply into my eyes and very gently and casually asked me: "When do you ever get off the stage?"

I was shocked at his perceptiveness.

"What would you know?" I replied.

"It's just that I've never seen anyone with so much energy to keep up a performance for so long. Where does all of the energy come from?" he asked.

"How do you know it's not really me?" I asked.

"I'm a performer, too," said Julian, "but you . . . you've got too much energy. You know, sometimes it's frightening."

Julian was looking deeply into my eyes. I kept looking away. Yet, with each challenging remark, I would glare at him and he would capture me again.

I finally held Julian's stare and tried not to run away.

"There's somebody there," I said, referring to the person I had seen in his eyes. "Am I here?" I had asked genuinely.

"Yes, you're there," said Julian reassuringly.

He touched my hair. I pulled away.

"*It* burns me," I explained. "All touch is pain."

"I don't want to hurt you," he said gently.

Julian had asked me about my experiences in early childhood. I had tried, but couldn't tell him the secrets that held together the walls that were both my prison and my protection. I tried instead to explain things to him in evasive and symbolic terms, then gave up and hid behind the relating of the tragic early childhood events for which I had felt nothing. Unintentionally I was leading him in the wrong direction for the answers he sought.

||||

JULIAN FELL VICTIM to my own hopelessness, seeing that I was unable to climb out of the pit he sensed I was in and not knowing how to get the answers that might help me out. His frustration and his caring disturbed me.

I disappeared to a city two hours away. After two days I returned and phoned Julian.

"Where are you?" he demanded.

"I'm here, just down the road from you," I said, and gave him the details of where I'd been and how I'd now landed a position teaching English in exchange for accommodation in the attic of a student house belonging to a local language school.

I took time out to lock myself in my newfound attic room, alone. I began again to have night terrors, waking up yet being unable to call the room back to the image of its true reality. I watched the events around me as though in a picture theater watching a 3-D movie. I was terrified. The fear, stuck in my throat, escaped in nothing more than a series of stifled, whimpering screams. Nobody else heard.

In one dream, my little brother had been tying up seven small kittens. He was tying their legs together so they could not run and then tying their necks back to their legs so that they could not breathe or move for fear of cutting their own throats. I tried to reach out to stop him as he laughingly threw the first of the kittens over a high brick wall where I could not get it. I felt myself pulled from behind. My mother was pulling me backwards by the hair. I fought desperately to save the kittens, but to no avail, as my head came thumping down upon the wall.

Whenever I became Carol, my true self had always been

symbolized by a kitten. This was my sense of self when the real Carol had taken me home to her house like some stray kitten she had found in the park. I had once found a bag of seven kittens dumped by the side of a creek and had brought them all home where I hid them in the garage, just as I had slept in people's garages later. In my mind each kitten was to stand for a color of the rainbow, and each color of the rainbow was to stand for the different types of feeling people had, which were so evasive within me.

The first feelings I had ever had for someone I recognized as a separate person were for my little brother. In the dream, Tom's action of tying up the kittens and throwing them over the wall out of my reach was an expression of how my fear of feeling had caused me to tie myself up. Throughout my life, I had thrown this helpless self out, beyond the wall, into "the world," under the disguise of Carol.

Willie was the protector of this self, he tried to save the helpless kittens. Willie's fighting ability, however, was stopped before it could save them from my mother's actions, which had left the kittens to be thrown out into "the world" whether they were prepared for it or not.

I was furious at Julian for making me feel. I had decided that feeling things was quite dangerous in too large a dose, and I spent more and more time on my own.

It was too late to undo the ability to feel, and I now found it harder and harder to hold on to the characters of Carol and Willie. Since being on a special diet to avoid food and chemical sensitivities and to maintain a steady blood-sugar level, I was stabilizing physically. With this came the loss of the characters, some of the energy for whom had been fueled by the anxiety-provoking effects of allergic reaction. I could still act, but I could no longer shut myself out as before. Though partially controlled, however, my hypoglycemia remained a slave to my emotions. However, there was no turning back in the face of a new realization. It began to dawn on me that my fear was not fear of emotion, but a reaction to it.

The feelings brought to the surface by the stranger in

Wales were not going to lie down and die. It was too late to turn the clocks back, and Julian continued to stoke the fire.

In a second dream I saw my grandfather.

Since before my grandfather had died, I had had a recurring dream. I was walking alone through a void, surrounded by hills. Suddenly I heard a roaring sound, and huge ocean waves came gushing fearsomely over the hills from all directions, covering me instantly without warning. I held on desperately to a pole in the middle of the barren land where I had been standing. I closed my eyes tight. I could not breathe. I could not scream. I felt the crushing feeling, and the immensity of the ocean swallowing me up. As the tide went out, the ocean gushed back over the hills as instantly as it had come. I clung terrified to the pole, too afraid to move. I think that's how my real self experienced emotion for most of my life.

In my second dream, I was surrounded by a high wall. My grandfather was leaving through a hole in the wall, and I reached out to try to stop him. I waited until he had left, then went after him.

After I climbed through the hole, I found myself again, as before, in a barren land. I called out. My voice was hollow, like an echo. Nobody answered.

I ran back through the hole in the wall, and my mother grabbed hold of me. I knew that she was going to try to make me stay on this side of the wall. I searched frantically for my way back to the barren land, but I could not find the hole and I was trapped.

I woke up unable to shake off the incredible feeling of vulnerability I felt, and no longer felt so secure being alone. Whether I liked it or not, at the age of twenty-six I was being made to stay in "the world."

||||

SINCE THE NIGHTMARES began, I felt more afraid indoors than I did outdoors, especially at night. I began to go walking through the snow and the leaves up in the hills at night.

Up in the forest, in the snow, it was not as dark as one might think. The snow reflected a whiteness all around; it seemed more like early dawn, the time I used to go and visit my grandfather.

I lay in the snow in my raincoat. My feet were soaking wet where the snow had got in through the holes in the soles of my boots. In a quiet little voice I sang to myself in my bed in the snow and wished I had the courage to ask Julian to come and sit with me to protect me. I thought of the stranger from Wales and wondered how I'd ever go back to see him again after the huge journey I had made through my own soul. I sang some of the songs I had written and bathed in my own sense of security.

It was time to say goodbye to Julian. Out of the blue I phoned up late at night to say I was going first thing in the morning.

"Stay right there. I'll pick you up," he said.

I arrived at the children's home where I had stayed almost two months before. Insecure, I kept my coat on and my bag by my side. I had a door. It was safe to try to let myself be there.

Julian touched my hand. I linked my fingers through his as though this was my grandmother's crocheted cardigan. He tried to look into my eyes. We were both there. The rest of the people in the room seemed to disappear. Our feet were touching. I was again painfully aware of the closeness but kept reassuring myself that it was safe.

This self-reassurance was something new. Willie had gone from being a prison warden to a psychiatrist to a genuine mother who spoke my own language. I finally felt at home within myself within "the world."

"I've got to go," I said.

"I'll walk you to the door," said Julian.

For the first time, I reached out to hug *him*. I stayed with the feeling, telling myself reassuringly: "It's okay, it's okay, I promise we can go if it hurts too much."

Julian lifted my chin and looked into the eyes of my peacefully smiling face.

"I'm here. Are you there?" I asked.

Julian smiled.

My fear had got the better of me. I hurriedly and bluntly said "Bye" and turned, my gaze fixed to the ground as I started to walk away from the house.

"It's okay," I said to myself. "See, I said we could go if it hurt too much."

I turned and walked back over to Julian. I raised my head and looked sadly into his eyes the way I had looked at my grandfather when I had felt his realness slipping away from me. Julian didn't slip away. Tears rolled down my face, and I smiled peacefully, so proud that I had found the strength and trust to let him see my feelings and to let them come out.

"I'll miss you," I said, sniffling.

"Just come back one more time," said Julian.

"Perhaps," I replied.

"Just come back one more time," Julian repeated.

I hugged him once more and walked hurriedly across the lawn to the waiting car.

||||

MY RUCKSACK ON my back, dressed in my black coat and hat, I stood at the corner of the motorway and hitched a lift to the station that would take me out of Germany. I boarded the train as I had originally boarded the ferry—alone—and said goodbye to Germany as the train crossed into Belgium.

The train stopped across the road from the ferry that would take me back to the UK. I needed to run. I needed distance. Julian was far away now, but the me I'd found and been able to hold on to had danced in the light long enough to know that this was the way out.

There was nowhere in particular to go, but the ocean seemed like the place to be. I'd face my emotions symbolically and realistically and bring the two realms of awareness together at some point. I headed for Wales.

I arrived at the home of the Welshman. He'd returned to

the UK after three months away, and I went with his father to pick him up.

It was a very long drive, and his father did most of the talking.

"My son's a bit strange, you know, Donna," he said.

"No, he's not," I replied.

"Please don't tell him or his mother I told you," he went on, "but he's a funny sort of retarded, you see."

I smiled inwardly to myself, remembering how the Welshman had told me all of this himself, yet his parents thought he didn't understand. I remembered how he'd told me that his father had helped him get into the job he was in, and about the problems he had with friendships, emotions, and words.

"He had meningitis as a baby and it affected him," the father explained. "Sometimes he does funny things."

"There's nothing wrong with him," I put in. "He's just like me."

||||

THE WELSHMAN'S NAME was Shaun, and Shaun was quite clearly drunk. Climbing into the front seat of the car, he hardly looked at me. He had known I was coming, and the quick but silent glances he shot across the car spoke louder than words.

We were stuck in traffic on the motorway, and Shaun got out of the car without warning. He was oblivious to his father's shouts and made his way to the side of the motorway and took a leak.

His father turned to me and said sorry, and it occurred to me that he thought I must have been embarrassed by his son's behavior.

"What for?" I asked, for it hardly seemed odd to take a pee when a person needed one.

"He's a bit weird sometimes, our Shaun," he said, hoping to make up for the embarrassment, which was his and not mine.

Shaun climbed back into the car as it continued to move along the motorway but this time he climbed into the back. He sat there unable to look me in the eye, and instead of feeling threatened by my having understood him I now felt the need to say I had. Silently I said it in a look, and for that moment Donna had spoken, albeit silently, in "the world." We touched hands, and I felt chilled and thought how lucky he was to be drunk at that moment. We still didn't look at each other.

IIII

BACK AT HIS parents' house, Shaun went straight out. He returned hours later drunker than he had left, having hitched a lift back from the next town. I had been staring straight at the ceiling and sat bolt upright as though given an electric shock. Jolted suddenly from the secure predictability of my world under glass, I stared silently at the figure who had entered the room.

Shaun's face stared silently back at me, and in his eyes I saw the same look I'd given my grandparents many years ago. It was a look that spoke of being a thousand miles away with no way back.

Shaun started to leave again, and I told him to wait and take me to the station. He had brought some gifts back from his trip, as had I. Without saying anything, he had placed a stuffed leather camel by my bag. I looked at it and thought how this creature drifts through the desert with no particular place to go or be. I moved it away and, picking up my bag, turned my back on it to go.

"Sorry he's like this," said his parents, who seemed angry at their son's distant behavior. The fact that he was like this had clouded these same characteristics in myself.

"It's okay," I said, "I understand."

They continued, and I saw echoes of my own mother's shame and excuses. The words "Don't worry about her, she's crazy" rang in my ears, and I spat out the words: "I understand why he's like this. It's not him. It's not me. It's both of us. We're both like this," I said. I didn't have a translation for this big word *this*, but I knew it felt like death.

||||

SILENTLY SHAUN DROVE like a maniac to the station, his eyes riveted on nothing in particular. He was rigid and trembled violently. He hit the brakes, and his eyes were desperate as he reached for my door and pushed it open. His shaking hands gripped my arm as I went to run from the car, and he grabbed a piece of scrap paper and a pencil.

He was shaking so much he couldn't write. The pencil tore through the paper, and the battle he was having with himself showed in his eyes, which were filling with tears of frustration.

He finished making scratches on what was left of the paper and forced it roughly into my hand and closed my fist around it.

"Go. Go before something happens," he said, and shoved me away before slamming the door and speeding off.

I stood on the platform shaking, afraid to look at the note. It crossed my mind to throw it away. It was all too much. It was all too familiar. It was all too me.

||||

THE TRAIN WAS going to nowhere in particular as far as I knew. All that mattered to me what that I was going away from here. The colors were too much. The lights were too much. The people and their sounds were too much. I curled up in a corner and turned to the wall and let it all die away, the note screwed up in my hand.

I got to the end of the line and realized I had no ticket. I crossed the platform, jumped onto the tracks, and walked along in the darkness beside a tall wire fence. "What are you doing?" I heard myself say. I answered by scrambling up the embankment with the intention of finding out where I was and where I was going to.

I stopped at a bus stop, happy to be alone in a quiet place; a nobody nowhere. I realized I was still holding the note.

Under the street light, I unraveled the crumpled paper. The words upon the page defied the roughness of the writing. "You were the best friend I had waited my whole life for. Stay in touch," it read. There was a Shaun in that note. There was a Donna in that note. And, little did I know, there was a word to describe why, that would tell me there were many more like me out there who may or may never make it down the path we both had found. Ours was a path with black holes everywhere you stepped. Into each one you could fall down and down for what always seemed like a deathly forever. This was a path where we walked alone and smiled our well-trained smiles as the world passed by and we looked out from what felt like a world under glass.

||||

I GOT BACK in touch with Shaun. He found it very hard to talk. He phoned me back four times, stuttering, breaking off in mid-sentence and "talking in poetry." On the fifth call he told me how much trouble he'd had since he'd met me. His boss had become very concerned that he was crazy. He'd isolated himself more than usual and lived in his thoughts.

"I've got a problem," he said to me on the phone between lengthy pauses. "I'm in love with you," he finally managed, and the line went silent on both ends. "The problem is," he finally went on, "I feel it's going to kill me."

"I know," I replied.

That was the last Shaun had managed to communicate. I have never seen or heard from him again. For some time, neither have his parents. He simply disappeared as I so often had. Perhaps he went to the ocean.

||||

I FOUND A flat in London and a job as a secretary. It was just what I needed: the flat on the top floor all to myself, the job with an office just for me. I was working in the administration section of a major hospital for an impossible boss who acted like something out of a cartoon. During lunchtime I would look at birds and squirrels on the hospital grounds, tear leaves apart, and go to the local library.

At home I had bought a cheap plastic typewriter and begun to type. I began with the center of my world as far back as I could remember. The nights got longer as one page rolled into the next and I relived each moment, staring straight ahead and letting the words come from my fingers.

I was searching inside myself for a word for what I had shared in common with Shaun. As the pages mounted up, so did my visits to the library, where I buried my head in books on schizophrenia and searched desperately to find a sense of belonging within those pages that would give me a word to put to all of this.

Suddenly it jumped out at me from the page. It was the first time since my father had said it four years ago that I'd heard the word. "Autism," it read, "not to be confused with schizophrenia." My heart jumped, and I shook. Perhaps this was the answer or the beginning of finding one. I looked for a book on autism.

There upon the pages I felt both angered and found. The echoed speech, the inability to be touched, the walking on tiptoe, the painfulness of sounds, the spinning and jumping, the rocking and repetition mocked my whole life. My head swam with images of the abuse that had been my training. The necessity of creating the characters had torn me apart but saved me from being a statistic. Part of me had complied with my training, the other part had made it through twenty-six years with a private, cut-off world intact.

||||

I WANTED AN opinion once and for all as to why I was like this. I decided to take my book to a child psychiatrist who could read it and tell me why. During my lunch break I asked for directions to the child psychiatry department of the hospital. I looked for and found a door with the appropriate label on it and knocked.

"I've written a book," I said to the professional behind the desk, "I want you to read it and tell me why I'm like I am," I told him.

The psychiatrist was taken aback and asked me what the book was about. I told him how I'd been called crazy, stupid, disturbed, and just plain weird, and that my father had told me people had said I was autistic.

"Well, the way you've presented me this book seems rather autistic," he commented. He asked why I'd chosen him to read it, and I explained that I'd simply looked for a door with the right label on it.

It wasn't long before I heard back from this doctor. He was quite taken by the book and wanted a specialist on autism to read it. He asked me if he could send it on. It hadn't occurred to me that it might be published, and I was scared. He pointed out that there were many children who had had experiences like mine and that my book might be important in understanding them. I had wanted to burn it. I had written it for myself and had wanted just to read it back and see my life consistently and see that my life had belonged to me. I also wanted to know why it had all happened because, although I'd found many answers, I hadn't yet worked out why it had all happened in the beginning.

The response that came back was overwhelmingly supportive. My book had, it seemed, portrayed what is typically seen in autistic children, though I had no doubt done better at overcoming my difficulties than many ever would. I was encouraged to send the book to a publisher.

At home my mind worked overtime as I slept. The characters were out of hiding and so was I. My fear of sleep was still strong, and the dreams it threw me into were almost more than I was ready to see.

I was dreaming. A mouse ran across the bare floorboards of an empty attic. Another mouse followed. Fighting the awareness of what I knew, my face remained blank, my expression oblivious. A man went to kill them.

"No," I screamed suddenly, "you can't. They're not

mice," I said finally, "they're kittens. Please, can we feed them?" I asked pleadingly.

He opened a cupboard door, and tins of food fell out onto the floor. I opened one of the cans and called the kittens. He went to touch one as it approached.

"No," I shouted, "if you touch them, they will die."

As they ate, they began to grow. I felt torn about feeding them. What would happen to them after I was gone and there was no one else to feed them again? I thought. It is better never to be fed than be fed and have it taken away again. The man looked at me crouched down on the floor.

"I must tell you," I said almost in a whisper, "there are more of them. There are seven."

I woke up in a sweat and paced around the room. The words had been freed by the book, and now their meaning was, too. I cried and rocked and told myself it was okay to *be*.

I went out and got a tin of cat food and sat it on the side table next to my bed. Although I had no real cat, it was to be a symbol that I would commit myself to feed and care for the kittens that represented myself. It was a way of showing I meant this commitment in "the real world," not just in mine.

||||

YEARS BEFORE, I had found a small kitten in an industrial waste-bin. I had taken it home, but I didn't know how sick it was or how to care for it properly, and it had died. I was about to be revisited.

I looked at the tin of cat food in the lamplight and eventually drifted off to sleep. I saw myself as a teenage Carol in a corner chattering away to a group of friends. A rustling noise came from the large waste-bin nearby. Carol ignored it, talking faster and faster. There was a sense of urgency that nobody should take their attention away from her; nobody should notice the rustling from the bin. After all, it was probably only a rat or something.

A dirty little girl of about four in a torn dress emerged

from the bin in a scurry. Carol turned her back on the group, her body a wall between them and the little girl. Looking at the little girl, she said silently: "You've come home."

The little girl had backed into a corner, her eyes darting, poised to run.

"It's okay," said Carol. "I promise they won't come near us," she said, referring to the group. "I won't even touch you," she said to the little girl, and with that she walked away from the group without looking back. She walked with her hand held backward to the little girl and didn't stop to see whether she was coming. The little girl ran and took her hand without looking at her. The little girl's eyes darted back over her shoulder as they walked away together.

IIII

DONNA HAD GONE from being symbolized by a kitten to being recognized by my own mind as a human being, albeit a child. Carol had finally come back to the park and taken Donna home to "the world" after all these years. There was no need for the tin of cat food anymore. Donna would never again be anything other than a human being.

By now Willie had become a mother and an encourager, and Carol had promised to keep Donna safely away from groups of people. There was one more battle to overcome. Willie had to accept Carol.

By now I was developing a clear awareness of an "I" and was becoming aware that I would have to lose my dependence upon the characters as something separate to myself. I was, however, not yet ready to turn to people.

I came across a ragged little toy at a market. It was in a pile of broken toys with missing bits. It had a ribbon with blue spots on it and looked like a cross between a sheep, a rabbit, and a dog. It was fifteen to twenty years old and cost twenty pence. I bought it for myself and named him Travel Dog. He was to travel everywhere with me every day, just as the characters had. He was to become my bridge to living things beyond the wall of my own body.

||||

I NEEDED TRAVEL DOG, but having him physically next to me hurt me emotionally. It was a new experience, and I was unfamiliar with accepting the boundaries of my own body in relation to the world outside it. I hadn't been so aware of what this uncomfortable feeling was until I had become consistently attached to something that represented the feeling world outside me. I cried a lot and began to try to hug myself rather than lose awareness or attack myself with frustration.

Sleeping had become a bit easier with Travel Dog to keep guard over the darkness. But Travel Dog couldn't keep the dreams away, and the final battle was about to be fought.

||||

WITH TRAVEL DOG propped by my pillow, I fell asleep. Willie walked across the floor of an empty warehouse to where Carol stood next to someone.

"This is my client," said a teenage Carol, referring to the man who towered over her. The glib comment referred directly to the sense of domestic prostitution that Carol had been forced to live with.

"You don't have to live like this," said Willie.

"Oh yeah," said Carol mockingly. "Where else would I live?" she went on.

Carol was stuck in time, and not a nice time at that. It was time to show her that things had changed and there was now somewhere to go.

"You can come and live with me," said Willie as the male stranger stood there looking arrogant.

"How would I pay? I don't have any money," said Carol.

"You can do the dishes," said Willie.

"I can take care of myself," gloated Carol.

"I know you can," Willie replied. "Just come over and see if you want to stay. If you don't, you can go. The door will be open." Willie walked away without even looking at the

191

stranger next to Carol. Carol looked at the stranger, then at Willie walking away. Silently, without apology, Carol did what Carol did best: she followed.

IIII

I WENT TO the old tea-chest and took out my lace, my bells, and my buttons. Day in, day out, I sat for hours staring at them and categorizing them, then mixing them back up again. I was bathing in the freedom to be me. I had a solid sense of home and belonging within my own body. There would be no more self-abuse. There would be no more allowing anyone else to abuse me. Nor would I be pushed beyond what I could handle with my self intact. Willie would be supportive until I accepted those skills as my own and applied them to myself. Carol would talk when it was necessary to hold down a job until I felt I could accept those skills as my own. I knew I would one day find friends in "the world" to replace my attachment and dependence upon the characters as they faded away. Until then, I had Travel Dog. As Travel Dog became less of a protector and more of a comforting companion, I myself took on the dual roles of taking responsibility and being a friend. The war against "the world" was over. Nobody had won. There was a truce.

IIII

THE BOOK WAS finished and now I had a word for the problems I had fought to overcome and understand. The label would have been useless except that it helped me to forgive myself and my family for the way I was. Looking back through photos of myself taken over the years, I recognized three ways I had avoided looking at people. One was to look straight through what was in front of me. Another was to look away at something else. The third was to stare blankly ahead with one eye and turn the other one inwards. This had the effect of blurring whatever view I had in front of me. I laid my photos out accordingly and there I saw just how far back my problems had gone.

There were several photos with this third sort of gaze: a gaze that left my face looking somewhat divided down the middle. Unlike those where I looked through the camera and those where I avoided the direction of the camera altogether, these were the only ones that looked as though I'd noticed the intrusion of the person taking the photos. The photos had been taken by different people and spanned a number of years. What struck me, however, was the age at which "the look" first appeared. It was in a photo where I had been propped up on a chair. I thought I had been a few months old; certainly no more than four months. As it turned out, the photo had been taken by my uncle when I was several weeks old. The look, however, was unmistakable, especially in comparison with the others like it. One side of my face smiled with the eye turned inwards. The other side was blank and lost, the eye looking intensely into nothingness.

||||

I WANTED TO meet the other autistic people I'd been told about and was surprised to find out that they were few and far between, scattered across the country and across the world. I was in an even smaller category. I had become "high functioning." Nevertheless, I needed to meet others. I could only know where I belonged in relation to others when I had met the other side of society. I'd met a world of so-called "normal" people—the people I'd aspired to be like. Now it was time to meet people still trapped in the place I had come from and in some ways still was in.

Kath was a solid personality with whom I felt relatively secure. Her voice was rather flat and even, and the pace with which she spoke was easy to follow. She had long straight gray hair and darting eyes, and though I felt welcomed by her I didn't feel smothered by her involvement.

She had a son my age, and her son was autistic. When I met him, he was running his hands through colored beads. I didn't want him to say hello or ask me how I was. Those were words reserved for those who wanted to move in "the world," and her son Perry certainly didn't.

I sat on the floor nearby and took out a handful of colored buttons and glass fruit. I sorted them into groups, put my hand out to where Perry was playing with his beads, and without a glance and without a word, I dropped them. Perry caught them and did the same back. I remembered my first version of relating—mirrors—but this time there would be no one to say that my version of relating wasn't good enough. This went on for a while, and we began to modify the game. I had a bell that I jingled to myself and dropped it for him to catch. Like before, Perry repeated my gesture but added another noise to the jingle. I mirrored him. We began following one another about the place in turn, ringing the bell and giving it over as the game became more and more one between two people than one where we were merely incidental to the game we made the objects play.

I sat back on the floor, lining up the buttons in categories. Perry approached, picked up a button here and there and added them to my rows where they belonged. Without looking at him, I knew what he was saying. These "games" had always belonged to me. Now I saw that these "games" belonged to autistic people.

I hadn't noticed that Kath had entered the room. She was standing there silently as Perry came over to where I was, laid himself out, face down, on the floor in front of me, arms pulled up tightly against his sides as he shook with anxiety.

"Look at me," I said, reading the same action I'd seen so many times in myself. "Look, I'm daring to be touched." I had looked straight at Perry lying there as I had said it, tears rolling down my face as I read his behavior as one might a book. I had the tremors from head to toe and wished the Welshman was there to understand himself as I had come to understand myself.

I turned to see Kath crying.

"I never thought he had any language," she said. "Now I see he does. I just don't know how to speak it." She said she had never seen him look so "normal." I had never felt I'd understood another individual so well. "We think it is we who have to teach autistic people," Kath said. "Now I see it is us who have so much to learn from them."

||||

KATH WAS ALSO a teacher at a school for autistic children. It was time for camp, and she asked me if I'd come. I was scared to break the routine of my usual week. It was one thing to drift without direction when one was in total control. It was another thing altogether to break with an established routine to take up an invitation I'd had no part in making even if it was for just one day. But the offer was left open, and I was free to come for as long as I was able to cope and then could go.

I traveled by train, then bus, and then taxi to a setting in the midst of the countryside of Kent. The children were inside, and I was overwhelmed by the number of people. Kath said she'd tell them I was coming, but that didn't stop the usual "hello theres" and I gravitated to Kath and let her talk for me.

Not all of the children at this school were autistic, particularly at this gathering, but at the dinner table one girl in particular stood out as very familiar.

Anne was eight but the size of a six-year-old, with long blond hair and pale white skin like mine. More distinctive was her gaze: one eye staring blankly ahead, the other turned sharply inwards. She was seated at the table with her mouth firmly set around the edge of it as she explored its surface with her tongue. I looked at her and felt somewhat exposed.

Kath wasn't with her, and the other professionals were impatiently shouting at her in what I felt from her state must have been an unintelligible mass of noise threatening to get in. So these were the professionals, I thought, as I reflected on my mother's own approach. Looking at Anne, I thought to myself: I know where you are.

Getting Anne to do anything sent her into total hysterics, as one might expect from a child blind and deaf to the world around her and most likely also to herself. Yet something was missing. She had no form of comforting herself. I felt compelled to give her a consistent pattern; something to hold on to and use to calm herself down long enough for her to open her eyes and take a look at "the world." The threat of exposing this in front of other people seemed impossible.

Anne followed me about, and I headed outside for the space of unfenced-in greenness. Anne was chasing me as I avoided her; busy dancing upon her shadow. She began intermittently to focus on my shadow, and we chased each other back and forth in turn, both of us with our eyes upon each other's shadow and feet. I looked up to see a few teachers looking out at us through the glass of the kitchen window. Who's under glass now? I thought.

IIII

IT WAS NIGHTTIME, and the children were being put to bed. Naturally this wasn't an easy task when it comes to children who aren't used to being still and are not quite aware of what sleep is meant to be for. One autistic boy jumped up and down in the dark on the top of his bunk. Anne screamed in terrified hysterics as one of the professionals sat on the bed next to her tucking a doll in next to her, which seemed to horrify her all the more. Oh, those symbols of normality, dolls, I thought. Oh, these terrifying reminders that one is meant to be comforted by people, and if one can't, one is meant at least to feel comforted by their effigies.

The woman sitting on Anne's bed was screaming at her over and over again to shut up and propping the doll back in its place with every shove Anne made to push it away. It was more than I could take. Physically I moved the woman out of the way, moved the doll, and gave her my brush. Anne ran her fingers repetitively through the bristles listening to the soft, barely audible sound in her ear and the sensation on her hand. I began to hum a repetitive tune I used to hum to myself over and over again as I tapped her arm in time to the hypnotic tune. Give her something consistent to hold on to, I thought. There'll be all the time in the world for the experts to undo it.

Anne's crossed eyes were frozen in a dead stare, and she

became silent between sobs. I took her hand and made her tap her own arm as I had, the tune and the rhythm and the tapping held totally constant.

I heard a soft but audible rhythm coming from outside me. Anne was making the tune herself in her throat, and I slowly dropped notes of my humming and, as I expected, she filled them in as though they were and had been her own. Slowly I dropped out more and more of them until she was doing not only the rhythm in her throat but carrying the tune as she tapped herself in time. Then, for a frozen fifteen seconds, in that torchlit dark room, she completely uncrossed her eyes for the first time since I'd met her and looked directly into my face as she tapped and now hummed. I went to leave several times, only to have to repeat the process. What was important, however, was that as I left she continued to tap and hum the tune between short bursts of fear.

||||

THE SUN HAD come up on a new day, and a trip to the park was scheduled. Anne's screams came from a small room at the back of the hall. I walked to the door only to see the same tactics of trying to calm her down: screaming "shut up" into her face.

"I will stay with her," I said coldly from the doorway.

"You're welcome to her," came the reply, as though she were some sort of unwanted baggage the woman was glad to be rid of.

I took out a crystal I had with me and turned it in front of Anne's face. Anne grabbed for it, and I let her take it. She looked at it in her hand and I felt I could see glimpses of my grandparents in myself as I related to her through the object. I sang the old tune over and over, and Anne's hand went automatically up to her arm and she tapped herself to the rhythm and eventually joined in. We went out peacefully to the bus.

Someone grabbed suddenly for Anne, to pile her on to the

bus. In the confusion of children everywhere and verbal garble Anne again went into hysterics. Then suddenly her hand went up to her arm and she tapped herself, humming the tune. The bus started up, and she allowed herself to be strapped in. As she calmed down, the tapping and humming stopped. Anne was learning she could control her own anxiety and the level of overwhelming input. When we got to the park the same thing happened. She calmed herself down and climbed out of the bus.

I walked ahead across the grass. On tiptoe, Anne half-ran, half-stumbled as she made her way to where I was. She took my hand, and in unison we broke into a skip, swinging our hands as we went away from the others across the park toward the swings.

We both got on the swings. As we swung higher and higher, I remembered another park a long, long time ago and wondered if one day there would be a little autistic girl who would remember a person called Donna in "the world" whose hand she had taken to skip across the park.

Afterword

All people like to put things into categories. I do so with my buttons, ribbons, and bits of colored glass. As for people, I had only ever truly felt there were two categories: "us" and "them." Most people see things in these terms, too, but with different and more value-laden definitions.

I do not believe that being sane or intelligent is superior to being insane or retarded. Many times the insane person has turned his or her back on the often alienating normality that most people become conditioned to believe is a real and desirable goal. Similarly many retarded people are more in touch with the world, as they sometimes experience things in a much more sensual way than "normal" people. They overlook what are sometimes very corrupting complexities, and rely instead on simple instinctual reactions and responses.

In this sense I am both insane and retarded. I would add to this deaf, dumb, and blind; for, although the accuracy of this is being constantly disproved by what I am able to perceive or express, this was often the way I perceived myself to be, and behaved accordingly.

I have been with the mentally ill, the backward, and the physically disabled. I have also had the pleasure of being with others labeled "autistic." This was the only group who spoke my own language so well that I realized that much of what I had thought of as my personality was in fact my individual expression of many of the misunderstood and confusing symptoms of autism.

I do not think I am mad, though at times I was convinced by the beliefs of those around me that this must be so. Certainly, however, if I had the predisposition to become truly mentally ill, then my isolation within my mental prison would have caused enough stress to do this.

At times I have been considered moronic and stupid and, more politely, naïve. Such was the all-absorbing nature of my world as a means of coping with my terror of emotion. Yet these emotions were always the ones meant to be the most rewarding: the good emotions. Had my mother been kind and loving, had she tried to involve me or reach me, I'm sure I would never have had the freedom to find emotionally detached corners of the world from which to study and teach myself things through my characters. This freedom was born of my mother's neglect and rejection; yet, ironically, without this I believe I would never have been able to develop my intellect through the character of Willie and my ability to communicate through the character of Carol. It was these two things that helped me to live independently and saved me from a life in an institution. These two things also led me on a journey through which, piece by piece, I finally found the ability to stand as a feeling self in "the world." Thank God my mother was a "bad" mother.

Everyone has an individual personality and I am no exception. However, a problem—or the solutions to it—is not the same as a personality. What I know of autism is from my own life, and I cannot claim its relevance to anyone but me. That is for others to decide. Nevertheless, I have some views to share.

My brother Tom and I taught ourselves everything we know. In this way I saved myself from a large part of the accusation of being retarded *because* of my mother's neglect and lack of direct loving emotional approaches toward me.

This is not to denigrate the value of a loving parent in

helping such a child. Quite the contrary. If loving parents can try to stand objectively away from their own emotional needs and relate to such children always in terms of how those children perceive the world, then the children may find the trust and courage to reach out step by step at their own pace.

This, however, ought only to be an interim measure. Gain the child's trust and tell him or her that you accept who and where he or she is. Through trust he or she may develop interest in "the world," and at first this exploration should be on the only terms he or she knows—his or her own. Only once this is firmly established should you take the safety net away slowly piece by piece. This is the way to make a transition from the child's sense of itself *as* the world to a new sense of itself *in* the world so-called "normal" people share.

This method, in complete contradiction to normal interaction, is *indirect* in nature. In this way it is less all-consuming, suffocating, and invasive. The child can then reach out, not as a conforming role-playing robot, but as a feeling, albeit extremely shy and evasive, human being. The best approach would be one that would not exchange individuality and freedom for the parents', teacher's, or counselor's version of respectability and impressiveness. At this point I ought to make it clear that I am not espousing soft options. One must tackle war with war and disarmament with disarmament. I am saying that the war must be thought through, sensitive, and well paced.

The perceptual problems of deafness, muteness, and blindness are experienced as very real. They are, nevertheless, caused by extreme stress, brought on by an inability to cope with emotion.

Perhaps, as in cases of shock, this very real perception and the behavior it leads to are caused by oversensitivity triggering protective chemical or hormonal responses in the brain. Perhaps in something of a vicious circle this emotional hypersensitivity in turn leads to developmental problems that arise from the inconsistency of changes in consciousness, and leaves such children functioning on a far more sensory and subconscious level for most of their waking lives as well as their sleeping ones. My tendency to night terrors pointed to this. My constantly changing sense of time and space also indicates that some of this emotional insecurity arises from the drifting in and out of a dream state.

Certainly my situation was heightened by the effect of multiple food allergies. Untreated, severe food intolerances can cause brain damage, arising from both toxicity and malnutrition due to malabsorption. At the same time, metabolic problems may lead to an inability to adjust adequately to different foods, resulting in the sensitization that leads to food intolerance. It therefore works both ways. Severe food intolerance can lead to brain damage, but some forms of brain damage can also manifest themselves in food intolerance.

Phenol intolerance is an example of one form of food intolerance particularly associated with autism. Sensitivity to colorings, flavorings, and preservatives has been found to be associated with hyperactivity. Even when intolerance doesn't cause actual damage, it affects the body's rate of absorption of vitamins, minerals, and toxic substances and so affects the functioning of the brain. Since being treated for my own intolerances and deficiencies, I have been able to cope far better with the anxiety that set up a barrier to change, self-awareness, expression, and comprehension. I wasn't so much hyperactive as extremely restless. Recognizing my food allergies also stopped me being physically so agitated and restless. I began to find some sort of a rhythm and permanence within my own body, and this has helped in my acceptance of my body as belonging to me rather than something with a mind of its own, constantly driving me crazy. I have recently read that metabolic problems may be the basic cause of problems in between 8 and 20 percent of autistic people. The fact that most doctors have not formally studied the effects of nutrition, food intolerance, and vitamins and minerals on health has generally led to a shunning of what this area of health practice may have to offer, and this is unfortunate. I was lucky enough to be treated by a doctor who practiced natural medicine. However, there are some cranks out there in the field of natural medicine who don't know any more about this area than most doctors do and they give a bad name to those who do know what they are talking about.

IIII

HUMAN BEINGS ARE made up of three systems, which in the normal person are reasonably integrated: mind, body, and emotions. In some people, one of these systems is faulty and makes complete integration impossible. Three examples of this are, in my belief, mental retardation, physical disability, and autism.

In retardation, the mental or intellectual mechanism has broken down, constraining the normal expression of one's self through an otherwise healthy body and emotions.

In physical disability, body function is faulty and traps and constrains the expression of a healthy mind and emotions.

I believe that autism results when some sort of mechanism that controls emotion does not function properly, leaving an otherwise relatively normal body and mind unable to express themselves with the depth that they would otherwise be capable of. Perhaps before an autistic child is even born it is unable to receive or make sense of any message that says there is a connection between itself and its mother. This inability to comprehend closeness constrains the formation of attachments and inhibits efforts to make sense of one's environment in infancy. Without this, perhaps the child creates within itself what it perceives as missing and in effect becomes a world within itself to which all else is simply irrelevant, external, and redundant. The child *as* a world is no longer a person, and hence the child does not perceive the absence of emotional attachment until he or she begins to be imposed upon by a world that expects it, along with the desire to learn and to be part of things, which usually springs from emotional attachment and belonging. Nevertheless, despite the deficits, in the case of autism there is hope of reaching one's potential and overcoming some of one's problems, though the means of doing this in itself can create new problems.

As for the placement of schizophrenia among these three categories, I would place this at the opposite end of the scale from autism. A progression along this scale would range from truly emotionally detached, through autistic, to shy and distant, to normal, with schizophrenia placed on the other side of normal. The criterion for such a scale would be the degree of sensitivity of an automatic cut-off mechanism that stops emotional overload. In the autistic, I believe, this is underdeveloped and oversensitive and is triggered too easily. In the normal person, this probably only comes into action in extreme shock-producing situations and is short-lived. Perhaps schizophrenia is the breakdown of the mind that occurs when this ability to cut off is not sensitive enough to protect the mind from mental breakdown. This is why I believe that, while it may look like it, autism is not a form of madness. If anything, autism is an extreme example of a mechanism that acts to protect sanity.

Basically the solution I found to minimize overload and thereby to enable my own self-expression was actually to fight for, and not against, a separation between my own mind and emotions. This points to the question of whether we must redefine this response as an act of sanity rather than of madness, for it has, indeed, never been viewed that way.

To do this to myself, I had constantly to convince myself that there was nothing personal or emotional in what I was doing, and constantly to hypnotize myself in order to calm down enough to allow some self-expression; to reduce the stress and emotional resistance to the "sellout" I felt by admitting a need to communicate.

Perhaps, according to basic definition, this response is schizoid, but schizoid behavior is not the same as true schizophrenia. Look around you. Most people force themselves to do things against their natural emotional reactions.

We live in a schizoid society. This is alienation. I believe I was born alienated, and if not, I was certainly so by the time I got left behind in emotional development at about the age of three.

Autistic people are not mad, not stupid. They are not fairies, not aliens—just people trapped in invisible, crippled emotional responses. At the same time, it would be misleading to think that such people do not feel. A physically disabled person can move, but the messages to the brain are faulty, resulting in often inappropriate movements. In my case, my mind knows that affection and kindness will not kill me, yet my emotional response defies this logic, telling me that good feelings and gentle and loving touch can kill me or at the very least cause me pain. When I try to ignore this message, I go into what would seem to be a state of shock, where what's coming in is either incomprehensible or has no significance. This state leads to my emotions committing suicide, leaving me without physical or emotional feeling and with a purely robotic mental response—if that.

At the same time, subconscious will to escape this emotional prison is probably why such people are sometimes thought to be geniuses. Perhaps they find a bit of light in the darkness, and clutch at it as though it were the way out. If only it was.

||||

IF YOU CLOSE your eyes and try to lose all conception of night or day, light or darkness, time or space, you may be able to grasp just how unreal time and space actually are. They exist within clocks and calendars and the structures created by people who have been agreed upon as a shared conception of such things.

Einstein, who is documented as having had learning disabilities, taught us that there is a point at which all things can be broken down into the minutest of parts and that it is at this point that something can pass through a seemingly solid object. He also believed in the ability to move through time and space, which made a mockery of the seemingly dependable idea that there is any sort of absolute reality.

People think of reality as some sort of guarantee they can rely on. Yet from the earliest I can remember I found my only dependable security was in losing all awareness of the things usually considered real. In doing this, I was able to lose all sense of self. Yet this is a strategy said to be the highest stage of meditation, indulged in to achieve inner peace and tranquillity. Why should it not be interpreted as such for autistic people?

I rejected all contact because it robbed me of the security I found in my ability to lose myself through color, sound, pattern, and rhythm. This was no great paradise, but it was my sanctuary from the fear of death that feeling good emotion gave me. For those who would talk of alienation, I was, as far as I can make out, born alienated from the world, and later became alienated from myself in responding to "the world."

I have learned that the world also makes nonautistic people this way. Perhaps in some strange way I started at the end and tried to work my way back. T. S. Eliot wrote, "In my beginning is my end" and "In my end is my beginning." Strangely, it was Bryn who had me read that poem. Perhaps he had found answers for himself long before I battled hard and long to get there. For what does life teach us but that there are no guarantees, and that vulnerability is our downfall? What does life ultimately teach us but to rely upon ourselves, for in the end we will quite likely be alone.

Through his paintings, Vincent van Gogh tried to capture the meaning of a three-dimensional world on a two-dimensional surface. Through his paintings he tried to teach people to look beyond the surface image of things and to see the true beauty in the individuality of things so often dismissed as ugly. He tried to teach people the beauty to be found in simplicity.

In the end, it is not knowledge that matters but the nature of a person's spirit. Alone, it is not the mind that strives for knowledge but the spirit that guides it. Untouched purity, innocence, and honesty of one's own spirit make up possibly the highest stage any person could hope to reach. Beauty in simplicity.

In the world, the emphasis is on complexity, yet it is misleading to believe that complexity cannot be found in simplicity. People who pride themselves on the ability to think complexly with their conscious mind often still have not found the ability to think in symbols with their subconscious mind. In this blind self-assurance, so many attempts are made by well-meaning people to drag children's consciousness into the so-called complexities of "the world" without first asking to what extent that world is worthy of them. Perhaps this is the real madness, naïveté, and ignorance.

IIII

FOR LANGUAGE TO have any meaning one must be able to relate to it. For me, when the directness of relating is too great, the walls go up.

This means that under overload conditions any of several meaning systems can shut down partially or completely, in combination or in isolation. Sensorially, this can mean that any one or any combination of the senses can become extremely acute. For me, this made some high-pitched sounds intolerable, and bright light became either intolerable or mesmerizing. Touch was as always intolerable. On a cognitive level, the meaning carried by intonation and gesture can be completely shut down, leaving the listener with no emotional cues. The meaning behind the significance of social rules can be completely lost (where it had previously been understood and cooperated with), and the comprehension of the meaning of words can drop away, leaving the listener lost as to both concept and significance. For me, my expressive difficulties were secondary and sprang from these primary inconsistencies in my perception of the world around me and in the complex psychological defense systems I created to compensate, which trapped me even more.

As autism is particularly characterized by difficulties in

expressive communication, I will set out some strategies I have used.

At best, a person in this situation can speak fluently only by tricking the mind into believing:

1. that what it has to say is not of emotional importance—that is, babbling;
2. that the listener will not be able to reach the speaker via words—that is, jargon or "speaking in poetry";
3. that the speech is not aimed directly at the listener—that is, speaking via objects or to objects (this includes writing, which is speaking via paper);
4. that it is not speech at all—that is, singing an appropriate song;
5. finally, that the conversation has no emotional content—that is, stating hard facts and trivia.

At worst, the stress of direct, emotionally loaded communication either blocks the brain's ability to retrieve all or any of the words needed to speak a fluent sentence or won't allow the process of articulation to begin, leaving the words echoing within the speaker's head. The frustration of this can lead, as I described, to the deafening scream of frustration that may or may not get out of the speaker's mouth.

The comprehension of words works as a progression, depending on the amount of stress caused from fear and the stress of relating directly. At best, words are understood with meaning, as with the indirect teaching of facts by a teacher or, better still, a record, television, or book. In my first three years in the special class at primary school, the teacher often left the room and the pupils responded to the lessons broadcast through an overhead speaker. I remember responding to it without the distraction of coping with the teacher. In this sense, computers would probably be beneficial for autistic children once they had the skills to use one.

The more predictable and calm the voice, the less emotional fear it inspires. Emotional fear, however, is a two-way street. Mildly autistic children may emerge as themselves in an environment where they are able to relax, though not enough to "lose themselves." I had to make my way up to this stage. In my earlier years, I was generally unresponsive to an unthreatening voice, and if I complied at all it would be automatically, with very little awareness of what I was doing. It was always fear that brought out the characters, and it was through them that I functioned at school. Perhaps a more severely closed-off child would learn to respond to a combination of predictability and unpredictability in a voice, though there should never be so much unpredictability as to send a child like this into irretrievable withdrawal. This is a double-edged sword. If it is too predictable, it will be tuned out, although the child will trust. If it is too unpredictable, it is hard to tune out, but the psychological barrier of distrust will be greater.

Laughing is no indication of response to a voice. Laughing can mean enjoyment, understanding, or fear. It can also be related to the very literal visualization of something said at some other time, as the thinking-through of what has been said may be very delayed. Laughing can be inextricably tied up with the overload the speaker triggers, at which point the speaker's words are little more than a meaningless hum of noise.

As an echolalic child, I did not understand the use of words because I was in too great a state of stress and fear to hear anything other than patterned sound. The need to hide the fear is such that not even the face is allowed to show it.

The development of my speech was fueled largely by the repetition of a storybook record and jingles on the television.

When I later used repeated phrases, it was simply because I sensed that some sort of response with sounds was re-quired. Mirroring, as with the matching of objects, was my way of saying: "Look, I can relate. I can make that noise, too." If echolalic children often do better than others, it is because, in their own way, they are trying desperately to reach out and show they can relate, if only as mirrors.

In consolation to those who have children who have never spoken, something I know from creating songs may help.

For me, the words were already in the pattern of the music; they sprang from it.

When I heard speech as only patterns of sound, my mind somehow read the meaning of the pattern (perhaps subconsciously or even psychically?) and I often responded as was expected regardless of not having consciously understood.

I believe that all thought begins with feeling. Such children have feeling, but it has developed in isolation and can't be verbalized in the usual way, and most people cannot hear with anything other than their ears.

An Outline of Language in "My World"

I am not suggesting that the meaning behind all of the repeated gestures I made is the same as that of others who use the same stereotyped gestures. However, though I spoke with the words of "the world," my gestures were the more important language of "my world."

Sometimes these gestures were purely for comfort, security, and release of extreme tension and frustration. Although at other times it seemed such gestures were self-directed, they were still an effort to communicate and make sense of "the world." This understanding had evaded me as I had not until recently reached out to it freely with my own good feelings consciously intact. Expressing myself indirectly and symbolically was the only way I could dare "say" the things that were "too important" to express in a more direct way. Such was the irony of my situation.

In the event that an understanding of the meaning behind some of these gestures may help those of "the world" understand this language and reach similar trapped and frightened people on their own terms, I have laid out a rough analysis of what such gestures meant to me.

1. **The matching or pairing of objects**

   Making connections between things. Showing that relationships between two or more things *can* exist. Seeing this objectified, through objects, in the most concrete and undeniable way. Seeing this and doing this again and again gave me hope that if the concept was possible, then it would one day be possible to feel and accept these relationships in "the world." I was always within this world of objects.

2. **The ordering of objects and symbols**

   Proving that belonging exists and giving myself hope that I, too, could one day feel this same special and undeniable place where I fitted in and belonged in "the world." Also, creating order and thereby making this symbolic representation of "the world" more comprehensible.

3. **Patterns**

   Continuity. The reassurance that things will stay the same long enough to grasp an undeniable guaranteed place within the complex situation around me.

   As surrounding circles or borderlines, these are set up as a means of protection from invasion by that which exists outside, in "the world."

4. **Blinking compulsively**

   To slow things down and make them seem like a more detached, and therefore less frightening, frame-by-frame film. Switching lights on and off very fast had an element of this, too.

5. **Switching lights on and off**

   Similar to above, but the clicking sound is an impersonal and graspable connection with things outside oneself, like bells and music. It gives the pleasure of sensation denied by almost all touch, and provides security. The more patterned and predictable, the more reassuring.

6. **Dropping things repetitively**

   Freedom. Proving that escape to freedom is possible. Symbolically this is the freedom to allow good emotions to touch you without pain, and the freedom to allow them out and not be so afraid of them from within.

7. **Jumping**

   Jumping from heights means the same as the dropping of objects, though it is less secretive. This action also gave hope, confirming that the concept of hope exists so that the feeling of it, which is missing, is, in theory, possible. It is also a way of getting one's whole body into a rhythm, as with rocking.

8. **Rocking from one foot to another**

   I always saw a foreboding darkness between myself and "the world." The fact that getting through this imaginary darkness to the other side would take quite a leap is possibly also captured by the preparatory rocking from front foot to back foot so indicative of someone about to take a running leap: "Ready, on your mark, get set, jump through the darkness to the other side," probably describes it well. Strangely, I was always too afraid to jump when other people tried to get me to. I once ran straight through a series of hurdles, letting my legs crash against them, as I was too afraid to jump them at the last minute.

9. **Rocking, hand-shaking, flicking objects, chin-tapping**

   Provide security and release, and thereby decrease, built-up inner anxiety and tension, thereby decreasing fear. The more extreme the movement, the greater the feeling I was trying to combat.

10. **Head-banging**

    To fight tension and to provide a thudding rhythm in my head when my mind was screaming too loud for me to be able to hum or to repeat a hypnotic tune in order to calm down.

11. **Staring past things, seemingly at something else**

    An attempt to take in what was happening around me while escaping my fear by experiencing a visual image indirectly. Looking at things directly often robbed them of all their impact and meaning. I managed to learn so much in my final year of primary school in this way, although the teacher had no idea that this was my only way of taking things in in any depth. Similarly, I would lose the ability to play music by looking at my fingers and thinking about what they were doing. If I looked away and switched to "automatic pilot," the music flowed and I could create.

All things must be indirect. I constantly had to trick my mind so it would relax enough to take things in.

12. **Laughing**
Often a release of fear, tension, and anxiety. My true feelings were too well protected to really show any experience of pleasure in anything so direct and able to be experienced and understood by others. Carol laughed all the time. Carol was the embodiment of my fear of feeling, presented as a reasonably socially acceptable, constantly laughing character.

13. **Clapping**
Clapping has always been a better indication of pleasure with me than laughter. However, clapping also indicated finality—the signaling of the end of one event or activity and the beginning of another. It could also be an attempt to try to snap myself out of an inescapable dreamlike state.

14. **Staring into space or through things, also the spinning of things or oneself and running in circles**
A means of losing awareness of self in order to relax or cope with boredom caused by an inability to express one's self or feel for the things one did. In a more extreme sense, it is a form of mental suicide used when one gives up hope of being able to reach out or be affected.

15. **Tearing paper**
Symbolically disintegrating the threat of closeness. A symbolic act of separation from others in order to reduce fear. I often did this when I had to say goodbye to anyone, as though I had first symbolically to destroy the closeness in order not to feel any sense of desertion or loss.

16. **Breaking glass**
Symbolically shattering the invisible wall between self and others. Is this the wall between conscious and subconscious?

17. **Fascination for colored and shiny objects**

Grasping the concept of beauty in simplicity. Also a tool for self-hypnosis, needed to help calm down and relax. Often closeness to particular people lives within these objects whether or not they were actually given by the other person. A particular color of blue always stood for my Aunty Linda, a bright golden yellow button stood for another friend, a piece of cut glass stood for the real Carol I met in the park, tartan stood for my grandmother, and so on. I had merely assigned them these connections because they captured "the feel" of these people.

18. **Hurting oneself and also knowingly doing embarrassing things to cause a shock reaction in others**

Testing as to whether one is actually real. As no one person is experienced directly, because all feeling gets held at some sort of mental checkpoint before being given to self by self, it is easy to wonder whether one in fact exists.

19. **Deliberate soiling**

For me, this began in a semiconscious state. It was, I believe, a subconscious drive towards conscious self-awareness and "freedom to be." It was an act of self-assuredly breaking free of excessive self-control through defying that behavior regarding which conformity and self-control are so demanded and disgust from others is so easily inspired. It was, at the same time, an expression of frustration at having to conform without actually getting any emotional reward from this conformity. It is an act of self-determination, proving that one can let go of self-control in exchange for control over external expectation. The self-assurance of "freedom to be" that one gets from this act gives one the courage to keep trying to reach out. I went through this once, when I again found the courage to try to come out of my withdrawal, and as annoying as it must be to parents, I must say that it was an important phase I had to get through in order to progress.

It is also a way of making one's surroundings symbolically part of "one's world," which is the beginning of accepting a world outside the confines of one's own body. From a body to a room. From a room to a house. From a house to a street. From a street to "the world."

20. **Safe physical contact**

That which does not threaten to hold or consume. Hair-brushing and tickling are examples of this. In particular, tickling forearms is unthreatening, as this is a less personal and more detached part of oneself. It is also less socially valued than, for example, touching one's face. For this reason, it carries less social significance for the person doing the touching. Hair, in this sense, also seems detached from one's body. Again, this is as close as one can come to the fine line between direct and indirect touching without robbing the recipient of all physical sensation from touch. Otherwise, all touch is either experienced as pain or tolerated as though one is made of wood. Quite simply, it is as though the spirit leaves the body there to be tormented by what others may think is a kind act of touching.

A few hints

The best way I could have been given things would have been for them to be placed near me with no expectation of thanks and no waiting for a response. To expect a thank-you or a response was to alienate me from the item that prompted the response.

The best way for me to have been able to listen to someone was for them to speak to themselves about me out loud or about someone like me, which would have inspired me to show I could relate to what was being said. In doing so, indirect contact, such as looking out of a window while talking, would have been best. This, however, would only work once I had achieved the ability to cooperate. In this case, this seeming indifference would actually demonstrate awareness and sensitivity to the child's problems in coping with directness. Furthermore, the child will be able to develop more of a self knowing it has reached out to the other person for the meaning in what is being said, rather than being in the role of a passive object being imposed upon at a pace it cannot keep up with when confronted with direct and often emotive interaction. After this consistently achieves the result of gaining the child's attention, methods of explaining things through visual representation could be slowly introduced. Called speaking through objects or use of visual symbols, it is a way of communicating with personal distance without having to be at such a physical distance. This visual representation is particularly important in explaining social relationships, directions, or abstract concepts.

For children who have not yet achieved the ability to cooperate by these strategies, I must, against my own feelings, suggest a strongly persistent, sensitive though impersonal approach to teach the child that "the world" will not give up on it; that it will relentlessly make demands of the child. Otherwise, "the world" will remain closed out. Teaching the value of what "the world" has to offer will probably have no meaning or significance, but the concept of a war that won't go away can force interaction.

In order to receive pleasure from physical touch, it ought always to have been initiated by me and I ought, at the very least, to have been given a choice. Again, very small children would need to be challenged to learn that they can choose.

When people didn't touch me I never experienced this as neglect. I experienced it as respect and understanding. When I came to them and sat in front of them with the hairbrush or put my forearm out across their lap to be tickled, I appreciated a freely and casually given response that asked me nothing about what I was getting out of the action. To make me aware that I had a want for something was to have robbed me of it, and my ability to feel and courage to reach out again would diminish.

When I spoke, it was important that I knew I was being listened to and that the listener understood the seriousness of what I was trying to communicate and the amount of courage it took. At the same time, the listener should not make me too aware of my own efforts. I was only able to do so by letting my conscious mind believe that nothing of any significance was happening.

In play and symbolic gesture, standing calmly by, without looking intently at me, perhaps even replaying my actions a few feet away from me without directing these efforts at me, would have confirmed understanding of what I was trying to communicate and given me hope and courage to keep trying.

Allowing me my privacy and space was the most beneficial thing I ever got. As much as many of the things I did were dangerous and as much as people could sense my isolation, this isolation was not from being left to my own devices. It stemmed from the isolation of my inner world, and only the unthreatening nature of privacy and space would inspire the courage to explore the world and get out of my world under glass step by step.

Most important, I didn't need to be loved to death, but at the same time I'd never recommend violence (which I see as quite different from punishment). My problems thrived on violence, which told me I was safe and no one could get close to me. The degree of violence required actually to change my behavior constituted serious and dangerous abuse. This causes damage to the abuser, who is the very person the child needs if it ever "comes out." I could therefore never recommend it. Nevertheless, if love won't work, try persistent, detached, nonviolent war. War must be met with war and disarmament with disarmament.

Love and kindness, affection and sympathy were my greatest fears. It was great that other people had them waiting for me, but the frustration of trying to live up to their unmatchable efforts only compounded my sense of inadequacy and hopelessness. Pity did nothing. Love, despite the fairy-tales, would only be thrown back and spat on for good measure. Caring would have been useful had it been channeled into an informed understanding of how to build a world I could have trusted enough to reach out to. Sometimes people must love you enough to declare war. The jump itself through the darkness to the other side was something I had to find the courage and ability to do on my own. As much as one might want to, one cannot save another's spirit. One can only inspire it to fight to save itself. If love can't inspire it, external fear greater than one's inner fear might, but I suggest one try love first.

Above all I would encourage those who have strived to help people like myself that their efforts are not useless. Responding in an indirect or detached manner is not synonymous with indifference.